ON FOOT IN THE GRAND CANYON

Cliffrose in bloom at Bass Camp (chapter 6).

On Foot in the Grand Canyon

Hiking the Trails of the South Rim

BY SHARON SPANGLER

FOREWORD BY
HARVEY BUTCHART

SECOND EDITION
PRUETT PUBLISHING CO.
BOULDER ■ 1989

Second Edition, First Printing

1 2 3 4 5 6 7 8 9

Library of Congress Cataloging-in-Publication Data

Spangler, Sharon, 1942-
  On foot in the Grand Canyon.

  Bibliography: p.
  Includes index.
  1. Hiking—Arizona—Grand Canyon National Park—
Guide-books. 2. Grand Canyon National Park (Ariz.)—
Guide-books. I. Title.
GV199.42.A72G738 1986   917.91'320453   86-4909
ISBN 0-87108-790-1 (pbk.)

Printed in the United States of America

The author expresses appreciation to the following: Dover Publications, Inc., New York, for permission to quote from John Wesley Powell's *The Exploration of the Colorado River and Its Canyons*, a Dover edition, first published in 1961, of the first publication by Floyd and Vincent in 1895 under the former title *Canyons of the Colorado*; Peregrine Smith Books, Layton, Utah, for permission to quote from Clarence E. Dutton's *A Tertiary History of the Grand Canyon District*, first published in 1882 and reprinted by Peregrine Smith in 1977; Alfred A. Knopf, Inc., New York, for permission to quote from Colin Fletcher's *The Man Who Walked Through Time*, copyright 1967; Red Lake Books, Flagstaff, Arizona, for permission to reprint the geologic cross-section chart from Larry Stevens's *The Colorado River in Grand Canyon: A Guide*, copyright 1983; Grand Canyon Natural History Association, for permission to reprint weather charts from *Grand Canyon Climates*.

All topographic trail maps in *On Foot in the Grand Canyon* are from the United States Geological Survey, United States Department of the Interior. The author has darkened or added the trail routes and noted additional features.

CONTENTS

DEDICATION

To the Grand Canyon and all
those dedicated to preserving it; and

To my parents, David and Diana Cooper
And to the memory of Aunt Pearl

"You cannot see the Grand Canyon in one view, as if it were a changeless spectacle from which a curtain might be lifted, but to see it you have to toil . . . through its labyrinths."

John Wesley Powell
The Exploration of the Colorado River and Its Canyons

"Subjects which disclose their full power, meaning, and beauty as soon as they are presented to the mind have very little of those qualities to disclose. . . . Those who have long and carefully studied the Grand Canyon of the Colorado do not hesitate for a moment to pronounce it by far the most sublime of all earthly spectacles."

Clarence E. Dutton
A Tertiary History of the Grand Canyon District

Some people can go around the world without seeing anything worth noticing. On the other hand, the great American naturalist William Beebe could write a long chapter on what he saw in a square yard of the jungle floor. Sharon Spangler gets a whole lot more from several days in the Grand Canyon than sunburn and blistered feet. In *On Foot in the Grand Canyon*, she has exhaustively researched and carefully written the most complete and reliable guidebook to hiking the trails of the South Rim. It's also an engaging personal adventure story, a good read for hiker and armchair adventurer alike.

Sharon lets the reader *experience* the inner Canyon with her and her companions, enjoy the sights, and learn with them about its natural and human history. In addition to a wealth of anecdote, she gives detailed trail descriptions and enough of the daily experiences and hazards to smooth the way for the tenderfoot, while including much information that is unknown to many expert Grand Canyon hikers. All of this is woven into a lively narrative that avoids the clichés and inadequacies of an attempt to rhapsodize over the indescribable grandeur of the scenery.

Hikers at all levels will want to carry this book on the trail and read it again after their trip to compare experiences. Armchair adventurers won't need to take a single step over the rim: *On Foot in the Grand Canyon* will give them a real feel for what it's like to hike in the Grand Canyon.

Harvey Butchart

I hope it's obvious to my readers that although many chapters in *On Foot in the Grand Canyon* describe first hikes on some of the trails, I've actually trekked these trails many times over the years. I've covered much additional terrain, too: the sacred Hopi Salt Trail, the Beamer Trail and Escalante Route, the Waldron and upper Boucher trails, additional stretches of the Tonto Trail, and explorations on the North Rim side.

This new edition contains updates, revisions, and expansions. I've changed my recommended return routes for Waldron and Dripping Springs/upper Boucher on page 5, because hikers shouldn't attempt a cross-country rim return from Waldron unless skilled with map and compass. I've added a second solo hike in chapter 8, with descriptions of the routes to Granite Rapids down Monument Canyon in a long footnote. There's a new appendix on weather, along with updated addresses and index entries and some minor corrections. *Trail directions and conditions and water sources remain essentially the same so far, but you should always check with the Backcountry Reservations Office about them.*

The Beamer and Escalante are really in a class by themselves, more for extremely seasoned Grand Canyon hikers, and I decided it's appropriate to leave them out. Please remember to take, treat, *and drink* lots of water; and I also now recommend adding an electrolyte replacement powder such as Gookinaid ERG to your water.

Safe, happy hiking!

Sharon Spangler
January 1989

ACKNOWLEDGMENTS

This book came out of my head and heart. But without the experience, knowledge, and help of many other people, what's inside my head and what I found in maps and books would never have been enough to tell the story.

First, I thank the folks who hiked with me and helped me to see the Grand Canyon through their eyes as well as my own. My husband, Bob Spangler, took photographs, helped me to remember things, encouraged me through the rough times, and, being an accomplished writer, offered suggestions to make the text read better. My other delightful hiking companions were Pat Hansen, Bill Whipple, Esther Johnston, and Jim and Janece Ohlman.

My deepest indebtedness goes to the Ohlmans. Without Jim's help, the book simply could not have been written. A geologist who's already hiked more than 8000 miles in the Grand Canyon, Jim was my technical advisor on geology, topography, trail details, and natural and human history. He reviewed every chapter for accuracy and redrew maps of the Boucher and Tanner trails to bring them up to date. Janece shared generously her broad knowledge of Canyon flora and fauna and her deep attunement to Canyon processes.

I'm also greatly indebted to Harvey Butchart, the dean of Grand Canyon hikers and author of three classics on hiking there: *Grand Canyon Treks*, *Grand Canyon Treks II*, and *Grand Canyon Treks III*. Harvey gave me invaluable help on trails, topography, and history and is an endless source of fascinating anecdotes. He also checked every chapter for accuracy. I'm deeply grateful to Harvey for having the confidence in my book to write the foreword for it.

Louise M. Hinchliffe, librarian at Grand Canyon National Park (GCNP) from 1951 until she retired in 1985, is a treasure trove of information and research know-how. She answered all my questions, no matter how remote or offbeat some of them might have seemed. Gale Burak, a seasonal ranger at the park and something of a legendary Canyon hiker herself, provided historical background and lively anecdotes. My thanks to both of them.

I also want to acknowledge the research help from GCNP Assistant Chief Ranger Charles Farabee, Backcountry Subdistrict Ranger Charles V. Lundy, Resources Management Specialist Richard L. "Rick" Ernenwein, and backcountry rangers Libby Ellis, Dave Stransky, and Robert Turan. Thanks, too, to Gail Udall Tobin and Dan Tobin for being sources of anecdote and transportation, and to my editor, Merilee Eggleston, for understanding and for applying a deft and caring touch to the manuscript.

And, finally, I pay tribute to our three wonderful dogs, Mollie, Shadow, and Sunshine, who, although not permitted in the Grand Canyon backcountry, stayed sweetly underfoot through every step of the writing, with patience, love, and boundless goodwill that made the many months of this loving labor even more satisfying.

Note for the second edition: On my second solo hike, in October 1986, only a few months after the release of the first edition of *On Foot*, I had the good luck to meet Helen Wells, a Grand Canyon veteran and photographer. Our friendship was immediate. Coincidentally, she had just read the first edition, and she astounded me by stating in the most matter-of-fact way, "I figured I'd meet you down here some day." I thank Helen for sharing her vast knowledge of the Canyon with me, which has enriched my subsequent hiking experiences (one of them with her), and for contributing her award-winning photograph of the Monument in Monument Canyon to the second edition.

S.A.S.

INTRODUCTION

I grew up in a suburb of St. Louis, Missouri, terrified of bugs and undone by the heat and humidity of summer. I was an indoors person. If anyone had ever suggested to my parents that their daughter would one day be hauling her own water, food, and shelter around the Grand Canyon, much less writing a book about that strange activity, they'd have laughed off the notion as preposterous.

But people change. I outgrew my dread of bugs, although not my tendency to wilt in humidity, and while living in New York City in 1968–69 developed an enthusiasm for walking, which can be a most efficient and agreeable means of transportation there. When I moved to Denver, Colorado in 1970, I began to walk in the Rocky Mountains. Thanks to the delightfully low humidity in the West, hiking became a major pastime.

I went on a river trip in the Grand Canyon in 1973 and became lovestruck over the Canyon. I went down the river again in 1978. Thirty-seven years old and newly married in 1979, I began to hike in the Grand Canyon with my husband, Bob. Then came another river trip in 1980, followed by four more years of hiking in the Canyon, during which we evolved from novices into seasoned Canyon hikers.

In October 1984, this book started spilling out of me. As it took shape, I saw that it was going to be a detailed, interpretive hiking guide, with our adventures woven in.

The Grand Canyon is an environment with special hazards. Its trails are long and punishingly steep. All but the four trails of the Corridor (chapter 5) and the Hualapai Canyon Trail (chapter 3) are unmaintained and rough. They often have scary exposures or are washed out or obscured by rock slides. Water is scarce and summer heat extreme. Lack of preparation can ruin a trip—or worse. Adequate preparation of body, mind, and gear enables the hiker to hike safely and to discover in his or her own way the power and beauty and mystery to be found below the rim. If *this* average hiker could do it, so can others!

Before the reader drops over the rim with us, let's set forth some bare-bones facts about the Grand Canyon. You'll learn a great deal more as you read the book.

All of the Grand Canyon is in northern Arizona. It was incised by the Colorado River, which arises in the mountains of Wyoming and Colorado and in 1440 miles drains a 242,000-square-mile area in these states and in parts of Utah, New Mexico, Arizona, Nevada, and California, exiting in the Gulf of California. The Grand Canyon is 277 miles long, from Lees Ferry to the Grand Wash Cliffs. It's about 5 to 18 miles across, averaging 10 miles, and ranges from 3500 to 6000 feet deep.

The Colorado River drops 2200 feet in its 277-mile course through the Canyon, alternately flowing through long, deep pools and plunging down short, steep rapids that are 1.5 miles apart on the average. Rapids account for only 10 percent of the length, but for a good one-half of the river's total drop in the Canyon. The river's depth is from 6 to 100 or more feet, averaging between 20 and 35, depending on water levels. The river's width varies from under 100 to about 300 feet.

Tributaries drain and erode an intricate, treelike system of gorges that feed into the main Inner Gorge cut by the river. The walls of the chasms drop in repeated series of cliffs, slopes, and terraces, depending on the hardness of the rock formation being eroded. And herein lies the central fact about describing hiking in the Grand Canyon: *Progress along the trail is marked by one's passage through the rock formations.* Elevations, mileages, hours-to-hike, and other conventions of hiking guidebooks do not apply well in describing hiking in the Grand Canyon or in giving the hiker an idea of what to expect. However, I have provided such data in appendix B. What is most useful is to get to know the sequence of the rock layers revealed in the Grand Canyon. You'll become familiar with them as you read each chapter, and there is a geologic cross-section chart in appendix A.

One final note of caution: Grand Canyon trail conditions and routes change over time. They may even have changed since we hiked them and I wrote them up here. Water sources change seasonally and some dry up. *Always check with the Backcountry Reservations Office for the latest information on routes and water availability.*

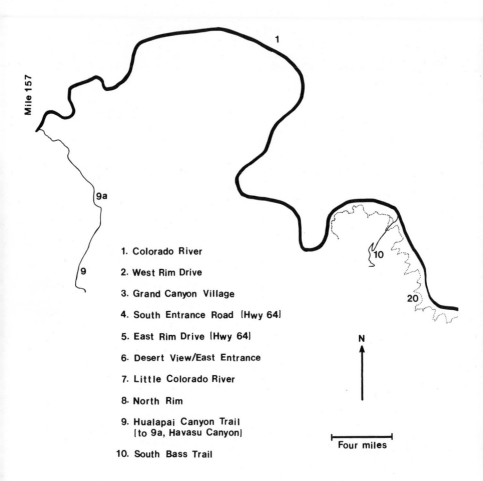

Mile 157

9a

9

1

10

20

1. Colorado River

2. West Rim Drive

3. Grand Canyon Village

4. South Entrance Road (Hwy 64)

5. East Rim Drive (Hwy 64)

6. Desert View/East Entrance

7. Little Colorado River

8. North Rim

9. Hualapai Canyon Trail
   (to 9a, Havasu Canyon)

10. South Bass Trail

N

Four miles

Trails Overview Map

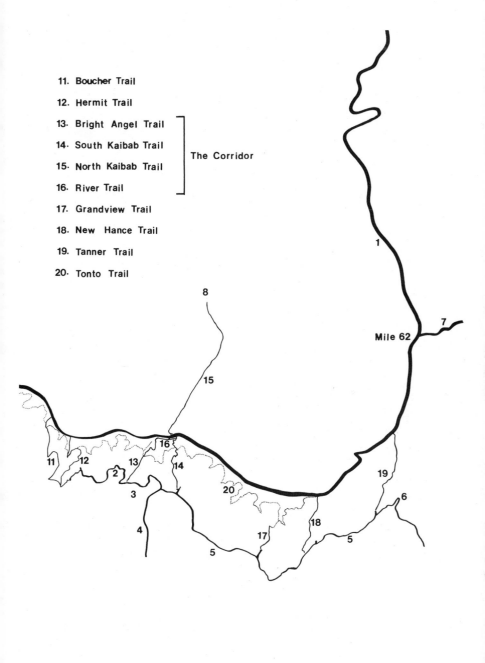

11. Boucher Trail

12. Hermit Trail

13. Bright Angel Trail ⎤

14. South Kaibab Trail ⎥ The Corridor

15. North Kaibab Trail ⎥

16. River Trail ⎦

17. Grandview Trail

18. New Hance Trail

19. Tanner Trail

20. Tonto Trail

8

15

Mile 62

7

1

16

11   12   13

2   14

3

4

5

20

17

5

18

19

6

5

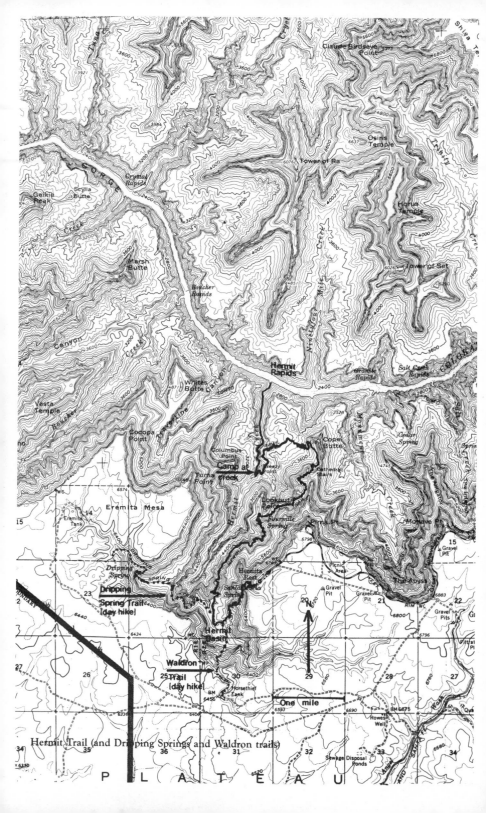

Hermit Trail (and Dripping Springs and Waldron trails)

CHAPTER 1

Hermit Trail
July 1979

July 3

Here I was, lurching and skidding down a steep trail cluttered with ankle-twisting, knee-busting, thigh-jellying rocks and boulders and wondering how I'd gotten Bob and myself into this. "This" was a backpack trip on the Hermit Trail in the Grand Canyon, our first one here. It was all my doing, and actually I knew full well how I'd gotten us into it.

On a six-day raft trip down the Colorado River in the Grand Canyon in 1973, I'd fallen in love with the Canyon. In 1978, before Bob and I were together, I'd gone down the river again, this time for sixteen days on the beautiful wooden and metal dory boats of Grand Canyon Dories. I'd done a lot of day hiking up side canyons to see fossils and Indian ruins and to frolic at fantastic little oases with waterfalls and swimming holes, and I wanted to come back. Serious hiking seemed like the next logical step.

Now I was questioning that logic—and my sanity. I wasn't exactly stepping along the trail. I was slipping and sliding on scree and negotiating some boulders on hands, bottom, and feet, or taking Bob's help. A natural athlete, Bob was moving down the trail with ease and agility. Several times he suggested I try to sight my next few steps in advance, to keep from pausing and tottering on one of those mean, shifty-eyed rocks. He meant well, but it annoyed me anyway.

"Easier said than done," I muttered, my face growing taut with concern.

I'd never have guessed that day that over the next few years, Bob and I would return again and again to hike here and eventually would become seasoned Grand Canyon hikers. This was a rough—not to say rocky—beginning. In our case, we started from a background of hiking in the Rocky Mountains outside Denver, Colorado, our home. It was useful experience, but we were about to learn that the Grand Canyon presented a far more difficult hiking challenge to us than the mountains did.

We had arrived the day before and headed immediately for the National Park Service's Backcountry Reservations Office (BRO) to pick up our camping permit, which we'd sent for many months in advance, and to arrange to check in on our return. This was a safety measure: if we didn't call in or show up at the BRO within twenty-four hours of our scheduled return, they'd start a search.

After getting our permit, we headed to Pima Point to look for our trail from the rim. Pima Point is located 6.3 miles from the Bright Angel shuttle stop along the West Rim Drive, the scenic road going west from Grand Canyon Village on the South Rim. In summer, private vehicles aren't allowed on the Drive because of congestion and air pollution. Instead, a park service concessionaire operates free shuttle buses all day.

Pima Point is the best vantage point to see the Hermit Trail because it juts out into the Canyon, whereas the trailhead, Hermits Rest,[1] 1.7 miles farther west at the end of the Drive, is set back. From Pima, we could see Hermit Gorge out to our left, plus part of Hermit Rapids at the mouth of Hermit Gorge and a couple more miles of the Colorado River downstream. We could see our trail switchbacking down to the Tonto Plateau 3000 feet below us and going west across the Tonto past the brown dot that was the ranger's cabin and the rectangular foundation lines of one of the structures at the original Hermit Camp.

The Santa Fe Railroad built the Hermit Trail from rim to river in 1910–12 as an alternative to the Bright Angel Trail at Grand Canyon Village, whose controllers charged one dollar for every tourist on it. The Santa Fe named their trail after "the Hermit," Louis Boucher, a French-Canadian prospector who lived farther west at Dripping Springs and at his copper mine in Long Canyon (since renamed Boucher Canyon). The Santa Fe opened a tourist camp on a ridge near Hermit Creek in 1912 and guided visitors down to it on mules. An aerial tram from Pima Point lowered supplies 3000 feet down to the camp—including, piece by piece, a Model T Ford.

The tram trip down took a half hour. In 1928, after years of litigation over the ownership of the Bright Angel Trail, the Bright Angel passed into the jurisdiction of the National Park Service and became the focus of tourist activity. The Hermit Trail's popularity declined, and Hermit Camp and the tram were dismantled by 1931 and the trail left to nature.

Bob and I were going to see for ourselves what fifty years in the Grand Canyon can do to a trail that is no longer maintained. Our plan was to hike on our first day down to see Hermit Rapids, 8.5 miles and 4240 feet below the rim, then back up Hermit Creek 1.5 miles to the campground at the creek for the night. The next day we'd hike out. It would be a too-brief introduction to Grand Canyon hiking, we knew, but it was all we had time for this year on this portion of our honeymoon trip in the West. Next year we planned to take the river trip here with Grand Canyon Dories.

This morning we'd assembled at the Bright Angel shuttle stop at sunup to take the "hikers' special," a nonstop ride out to Hermits Rest. As we waited for the bus, we looked again at our trail on the 1962 United States Geological Survey topographic map, "Grand Canyon National Park and Vicinity," and at my notes from the Hermit Trail descriptions in our two guidebooks: the Grand Canyon Natural History Association's (NHA) *Hiking the Inner Canyon: A Guide* (rewritten by Scott Thybony in 1980 and renamed *A Guide to Hiking the Inner Canyon*); and *Grand Canyon Treks* by Dr. Harvey Butchart, a Northern Arizona University mathematics professor, now retired.

During the ride to Hermits Rest, we and a handful of other hikers exchanged pleasantries. Yes, it was going to be a beautiful day for hiking the Canyon. And yes, this was the hottest time of the year for the trek, and the heat would place extra demands on us as we moved lower and lower. But that was hard to imagine, since it was cool and breezy here on the rim and most of us were wearing windbreakers or wool shirts over our T-shirts.

Twenty minutes and 8 miles later we arrived at Hermits Rest. We hauled our packs off, set them on the ground, called "Have a good one" to the others, and took a brief look at our destination from the rim. We could see the Tonto Plateau far below, still in shade. Slicing through it was Hermit Gorge, a dark, ragged gash down there—way down there. We could see almost all of Hermit Rapids, deep inside the black-walled Inner Gorge of the Colorado River. Above the Inner Gorge, in smoky blues, mauves, and pale golds alternating with purple shadow, terrace upon cliff after terrace upon cliff rose in great tributary canyons etching deeply back to the North Rim. In the quiet dawn light, all this vastness was utterly silent and full of mysterious promise.

We put on our packs and headed toward the trailhead down a gravel service road that led past public restrooms and a residence. About 0.2 miles farther we were there. A large brown sign with white lettering announced tersely:

> HERMIT TRAIL
> PERMIT REQUIRED for all camping. Permits issued at visitor center. NO PETS allowed on trails. NO FIRES. Stay on trails, no shortcutting. When in doubt, contact a Ranger.[2]

No hint here of what lay ahead. We were in a woodland of pinyon pines and Utah juniper trees that gave no clue that the Canyon was only yards away. We stepped onto the trail in the trees.

Abruptly the trail assumed what we would find in trip after trip to be the character typical of the wooded, blocky, cream-to-tan-colored cliffs of the Kaibab Limestone Formation, the topmost rock layer in the Canyon, on all the unmaintained trails: steep, treacherously jumbled switchbacks that I now found myself so awkwardly descending. This was bad enough going down, but it was so relentlessly steep that I found myself wondering, "What is this going to be like coming up?"

Soon the trail entered the Toroweap Formation, a mixture of sandstones and limestones so close in color and texture to the Kaibab that I couldn't tell the difference up close. In the distance, though, I could see it forming a short, steep slope above the rugged, sheer cliff of the Coconino Sandstone immediately below it.

We entered the Coconino now, still in the pinyon-juniper woodland. Its switchbacks were a little less rubbly, carved into the cross-bedded, buff-colored layers of what were windswept sand dunes 270 million years ago. There were remnants of the original trail construction: a steep, cobbled "pavement" made of slabs of sandstone set on edge, crosswise to the trail. In its day, I thought, the Hermit must have been a boulevard for mule-riding tourists. On later trips

I'd also see fossil reptile and amphibian tracks on some upward-facing slabs of Coconino alongside the trail. Their treadmarks – some distinct, some splotchy – marched purposefully across the panels . . . and into oblivion.

The trail through the Kaibab, Toroweap, and Coconino formations doesn't go out into the Canyon. It switchbacks generally southwest away from it, dropping down the east side of Hermit Basin, giving occasional views out into the Canyon. Hermit Basin is a pinyon- and juniper-studded bowl abundant in wildlife and wildflowers. From it, day hikers can take the Waldron Trail, which branches off the Hermit and goes south, eventually winding via switchbacks up and out of the Basin to the rim, ending at a fire road near a cattle tank called Horsethief Tank. There's no potable water enroute. Return the way you came, for about a six-hour trip in all.

Another day hike is to Dripping Springs, northwest of Horsethief Tank in the western head of Hermit Gorge. The 1.5-mile trail to Dripping Springs branches off the Hermit Trail to the west. Dripping Springs has water and is, I found in 1987, a bird watcher's paradise. To return, retrace your route, for a six-hour trip; or you can take the trail up to the rim, then around south to the road and from there take left turns at all fire roads to the Waldron Trail and return to Hermits Rest as described above. It's an all-day trip.

But I'm getting ahead of myself.

About an hour into our hike now and off the cliffs, we followed our trail north into Hermit Basin in the rust-red Hermit Shale. Bob and I decided to celebrate our arrival with a trailside breakfast. We found a pleasant spot under a pinyon tree, took off our packs and sat and ate our granola. It felt good to rest our quivering thighs.

Hermit Basin was an obvious and welcome stopping place. It offered, if not level ground (the Hermit Shale erodes into slopes), at least a respite from the pounding of the switchbacks above and a pause before the next formation, the Supai Group. The Basin was beautiful in the golden morning light. It was nearly surrounded by the cliffs and was alive with birds.

This was our first sit-down break. We'd paused along the way, of course, to adjust boot laces, fine-tune pack loads, and to drink water. Heeding the BRO's warnings about drinking often in the Grand Canyon, we drank. Since I get dehydrated easily, we exceeded their recommendations to carry a gallon of water each and instead each carried five quarts for today's midsummer hike in the desert.

After breakfast, we changed into shorts and slathered on sunscreen. We put on our headgear, which is essential under the desert sun. Bob wore a ventilated baseball-type cap. I wore a bandana and visor. Then we put on our packs and resumed our walk. The trail continued northerly and was steep and rutted as it formed or followed a runoff channel. Beside it were occasional wildflowers—lupine and paintbrush and the mostly spent blooms of larkspur and penstemon. We passed the junction to Dripping Springs on our left.

Suddenly we were going down a set of steep and rocky switchbacks. We were leaving Hermit Basin and moving northward down into the Supai Group, a multilayered formation of sandstones, shales, and some limestones. Now we could see out into the Canyon. Across to the west was the massive Supai wall above Hermit Gorge, topped by the Hermit, Coconino, Toroweap, and Kaibab formations. The Supai had a blocky, ledgy aspect and was predominantly shaded in deep reds and umbers. It was thicker than any of the formations above. Below it and about two-thirds as thick was the Redwall Limestone. It looked frighteningly sheer and was a brighter red than the Supai Group. The Redwall actually is a grayish limestone, but it has been stained red by iron-rich minerals washed down over it from the Supai's shales through the eons. Often the Redwall is streaked with black—organic "cliffwash" caused by leaching of overlying vegetation.

Down we went, moving northeastward high along the east wall of Hermit Gorge. We crossed a steep drainage with some deciduous bushes and room-sized boulders that had tumbled into it from the Basin above. The trail became semilevel to up-and-down. It was almost smooth in places. The pinyon and juniper trees were becoming smaller and more scattered. The Redwall would mark their lowest elevation.

Soon we reached Santa Maria Spring, still in the upper layers of the Supai, the only water along the Hermit Trail. (The map shows Four Mile Spring, but it no longer exists.) Santa Maria is about 2 miles from Hermits Rest. Here, the Santa Fe Railroad built a stone resthouse and a small corral below it for the mules carrying tourists down to Hermit Camp. The resthouse was open in front. Growing from planters at the base of the pillars supporting its roof were aged ivies. Over the decades they had grown up the pillars and across the front of the roof, where now they hung, heavy with rich green leaves, to frame the view of the Supai and Redwall across Hermit Gorge. Grasses five feet high were growing where the waters of the spring that weren't captured in the old trough trickled onto the ground.

Bob and I stopped here briefly to enjoy the beauty of the spot, the coolness in its shade, and the feel of the old, warped wooden benches, polished from the many bodies that had rested on them over the years. We heard the descending whistle of the canyon wren out over the gorge and the palpable silence afterwards. We didn't take any water here. We'd have had to purify it, as one must do with all but rainwater and campground fountains in the Canyon. What we had would last us all day. Tomorrow we would take water here on our way out, rather than carry a full load from Hermit Creek on the steep upward haul.

Suddenly the silence was broken. The day's scenic airplane and helicopter tours had begun. The Hermit area is a popular part of the Canyon for the tours.

We left Santa Maria Spring and now were back in the business of the slow descent of the Supai Group. It seemed to go on endlessly. The trail was level and fairly smooth. Or it was rocky and went uphill. It switchbacked downhill. It was obscured by rock slides and marked with cairns. It was moderate or steep in descent. Always it hugged the cliff wall on a narrow ledge.

The trail was usually wide enough for me, but it hung on the brink in a way that it hadn't done in the rock layers above. Most of the time I didn't dare look down to my left while I was moving. Though it had bushes and grasses and even some trailside wildflowers, the wall fell steeply away from the trail. Occasionally, the trail was wide enough for only one foot. My heart caught in my throat as I urged myself across these exposed threads. And *this* was once a boulevard?

Now and then we saw a lizard warming itself on a rock or scurrying across the trail. We met a group of hikers on their way up, resting under an overhang. They had left Hermit Creek before dawn. No point in asking "How much farther?" The rock strata told me that.

It was warming up now, but the Supai remained in shade. The sun wouldn't hit this wall until 9 or 10 A.M.

The Supai went on for nearly 3 miles. Seldom was there anything but air and a steep slope off to my left. There were, however, two saddles out to small points. From the placement of rocks in some clearings on the saddles, I guessed they'd occasionally been used as campsites.

At last we reached the top of the Redwall—and the sun. I had been worried about descending the Redwall. Looking at the raw, sheer cliff across the gorge, I couldn't imagine how its passage could be anything less than terrifying.

To my surprise and relief, the descent of the Redwall at Cathedral Stairs felt downright cozy compared to the Supai. It was rocky and scree-y like the Kaibab and Toroweap, but its switchbacks were snug in the cliff wall facing Cope Butte. Grasses and wildflowers clung to the edge of the trail. From the upper reaches of the Redwall, we could look to the east for the first time, through the notch at Cope Butte, at the retreating shapes of glowing walls, buttes, and peaks in the distance.

The descent was swift, unlike the passage through the Supai Group, but by the time we were out of the Redwall, our thighs were quaking and Bob's left knee had begun to hurt. The flesh under the big toenail of my right foot was tender from being jammed into the front of my boot. We were in the late morning sun, and we'd been on the trail four hours. Our progress had been slow because of me, and we were going to be on the Tonto Plateau in the hottest part of the day.

Now we were sweating and drinking more as we moved north then northwest down through the mottled-gray Muav Limestone in long switchbacks on the west flank of Cope Butte. On the Tonto Plateau, no longer so very far below, we could see small clots of hikers—those who had left before us and others coming up.

Once we were through the Muav, the ground sloped away from us on the left in rolling reaches of talus and shrub. Beneath our feet, buried in its own destruction, was the Bright Angel Shale. I had seen this lovely formation from the river. It had bands of light green, tan, and purple shales and sandstones. Here, though, the only evidence of it was to the north of us beyond the low saddle where our trail met the Tonto Trail. The rest of the Bright Angel Shale had eroded away to form the terrace known as the Tonto Plateau. At last we were on the Tonto! We met hikers and exchanged greetings.

And now it was full-hot in the late morning sun. There was no shade. The evenly spaced blackbrush of the plateau was only knee-high. I was beginning to feel headachy, probably from dehydration. This, in spite of all the water I'd already drunk. I drank more and ate trail mix for carbohydrate and electrolyte replacement. I took off my bandana, wetted it, wiped my face with it, and put it back on. The dampness felt good on my head. I was grateful we had each carried those heavy ten pounds of water. I knew we had plenty till Hermit Creek, if not till the river. Bob's head felt okay, he said, but his knee was getting worse.

Up until now the trail had hugged the cliffs, except in Hermit Basin. On the Tonto, it was finally in the open. We felt an urgency to get off it as soon as possible. We could see closer than ever the jagged, gray-black walls of Hermit Gorge and the somber, brooding slash of the Colorado River gorge, the Inner Gorge. These were the oldest rocks in the Canyon, the rugged, twisted, two-billion-year-old Vishnu Schist.

Harsh as it was in the heat, the Tonto Plateau afforded fast walking. We made good time on it, but we were growing tired. This trek, beautiful though it was, was painfully hard work for first-timers, and we were hurting. We could look up at the rim, a remote world now. I felt some anxiety being so far from it, and concern about the climb out tomorrow and especially about Bob's leg. Don't think about it. Stay in the present.

On we went, heading west. We passed the junction with the Tonto Trail coming in from the east and, less than a mile farther, another junction. To our right, the trail went to Hermit Rapids, bypassing the campground at Hermit Creek. To our left, the trail climbed briefly past the ranger's cabin on the ridge at the site of the old Hermit Camp, rounded a spur, and dropped down into the campground at Hermit Creek high in the Tapeats Sandstone.

We had to decide. Our plan had been to go directly to the rapids, then hike back up to the campground. But Bob's knee was less and less able to bear weight. Still, he had never seen a big river rapids anywhere, let alone one of the most powerful ones on the continent. I wanted to show him Hermit Rapids, wanted to see again for myself this grand, rip-roaring stretch of rolicking white water that I had surged through on raft and dory. If we didn't go now, we'd have to forego it until next year's river trip.

Bob said, "Let's do it." We worked our way down the brown

Fallen chunks of Tapeats Sandstone in Hermit Gorge

flake-pastry crust of the Tapeats Sandstone and into the creekbed, joining the trail that came down from the camp.

In the Tapeats, the trail was a delight. It went past small falls and pools. Grasses, ferns, flowers, seep-willows, and mesquite were abundant. In a narrows, house-sized chunks of the Tapeats had fallen into the streambed, and the trail was cribbed into the opposite wall. Then the trail entered the Vishnu Schist and the floor opened wider. We paused to look at the seam where the Tapeats Sandstone rested on top of the Vishnu. Here was a gap in time of a billion years, give or take a couple hundred million: the Great Unconformity. Twice or more in that billion-or-so years, great mountain ranges were lifted up and eroded off to a plain of Vishnu. The Tapeats was deposited on top of that plain in a shallow sea about 550 million years ago. In some parts of the Grand Canyon, the Tapeats rests on top of the Grand Canyon Supergroup, remnants of the second set of mountains, which themselves rest on top of the Vishnu, and in these places the Great Unconformity represents a gap of "only" 250 million years or more.[3]

A billion years vanished in the crack between the Tapeats and the Vishnu Schist. It was impossible to comprehend what that meant. Impossible even to imagine that the ages of the strata beginning with the Tapeats all the way up through the Kaibab Limestone totaled more than 400 million years. What did that mean?

Don't be concerned about it, says Colin Fletcher, author of *The Man Who Walked Through Time*, the story of his two-month trek through the Grand Canyon in 1963. If the numbers given by the geologists make you feel uncomfortable, he suggests, "settle for numbers that satisfy you. As long as they're big enough—too big to make much sense—their accuracy is not, for our purposes, all that important." It seemed like good advice, and I had also decided to adopt the same easy attitude toward the thicknesses of the rock formations, since each one varies throughout the Canyon.[4]

If it had been hot on the Tonto Plateau, it was an inferno in the Vishnu Schist inside Hermit Gorge, well over 100 degrees. The air didn't move; it clamped down around us. Mesquite chafed us. Insects buzzed loudly. On we slogged, hot and weary, drinking copiously and longing for rest.

It became sandy underfoot. The streambed fanned out and became tangled with tamarisk and willows, signs that we were nearing the river. We stopped to listen: we could hear the rumbling of the rapids. We were almost there.

And then, an hour after entering the Tapeats, we stood looking at Hermit Rapids. It was two o'clock. We had been on the trail seven hours. I was thrilled to be here but managed only a wan smile of gratitude and relief. Bob's face showed his pain, but his spirits lifted in the presence of such dazzling power.

We wanted to get as close to it as we could. Between us and the river was a white sandy beach strewn with polished boulders. All was in full sun, but the breeze off the water moderated the heat. It would be a rock-hopper to get to the water. Not with our packs on, we decided. We took them off—what a relief!—and placed them against the schist about fifty yards from the river's edge.

We took water, trail mix, and camera and went down to the river. Bob maneuvered himself onto a rock at the edge, removed his boots and socks and set his leg in the fifty-degree water. It offered relief, substituting the numbing pain of cold for the throbbing pain inside the knee. I took a photograph of him there, his hair blowing into a haystack in front of one of the haystack waves of the rapids. Then I took off my boots and socks, too, and cooled my burning feet in the river—but only for a few seconds!

Fortunately, neither of us had blisters, although our feet felt raw. The flesh under my right big toenail was red, forming a blood blister. It was painful to the touch. The nail would become purple and stay that way for almost a year until new nail pushed it out. I'd get "black toe" on several trips until I learned how to prevent it by sticking a double layer of molefoams on top of my outer sock, just under the tongue of my boot. This wadding behind snug lacing kept my foot from jamming into the toe basket of the boot on downhill grades.

We rested awhile at the river's edge, drinking, munching, talking. We shared our exhilaration at having made this trek, battered though we were. While we rested here, we had a treat that made us forget our discomfort: two river parties, each with several rafts, ran the rapids.

If the water level was right and if you lined up just right for the first drop, you could have a lively roller-coaster ride in Hermit down and up a half dozen big waves. I knew from experience that the waves of a rapids often don't look as big from the shore as they

A pontoon raft running Hermit Rapids

seem from a boat or raft. In the boat you sit on a glossy tongue of water that gathers speed as it slides down the first drop. (The average speed of the Colorado River in the Grand Canyon is about four miles per hour; in rapids, ten to twenty miles per hour.) If you catch the first wave at the right moment in its cycle, you climb up its tail and are over the top of it and heading into the next trough before the first tail can break over you. Of course, you need a skilled boatman or -woman to keep you centered on the waves. From the dory last year, that first wave in Hermit had looked fifteen feet high from trough to peak. It didn't look as large from the shore today.

We took pictures as one by one the rafts swept down the rapids, their passengers whooping exuberantly and yelling "Good ride!" I was especially delighted that Bob got to see them. I hoped it would help build his enthusiasm for next year's river trip.

Refreshed now, we put on our boots and explored the beach, looking at the rapids, the tortured crenelations of the Vishnu, the cloudless blue sky above. A scattering of other hikers turned up. We asked one of them to take a photo of us with our camera, with the rapids behind us. Bob took a shot of me with the South Rim in the background through the slit of Hermit Gorge.

We hadn't taken many pictures today, nor had we planned to. We carried only a simple snapshot camera for what Bob called "storytelling" pictures for our album. We had known we wouldn't have time this trip to try serious photography with his 35mm camera.

Too soon it was time to go. Our spirits sank as, reluctantly, we put on our packs and began the 1.5-mile trudge to camp. Back in the tamarisk, the air died again and the heat closed in. We felt as though we'd never had our respite at the river. Bob walked with his left leg stiff. In our inexperience, we had neglected to carry an elastic bandage that would have helped support his knee. It was a long walk back.

We arrived at the campground, situated on a small platform in the Tapeats twenty feet above and on the east side of the creek, at four o'clock. We were dazed and dispirited. We had walked 10 miles on grueling terrain, down 4240 vertical feet and back up several hundred, in punishing desert heat, under backpack.

We selected a campsite and spread out our groundcloth to claim it. Like most of the others, it was a dusty, sunblasted flat active with ants. There wasn't any point staying there for now. The sun and ants wouldn't be gone for another hour or so. Ants are diurnal, like humans. There were no mosquitoes.

Two couples socializing at another site invited us to join them. We took our packs over with us. The BRO had warned us that the squirrels at Hermit Creek have been known to chew right into a backpack in search of food, and we didn't want to risk leaving ours unattended. (In 1983, a seven-foot-high metal pack bar was installed at Hermit to enable hikers to hang their packs out of rodents' reach, but the nocturnal ringtail cats are said to have learned to climb that, too, so hikers are advised to suspend their packs from a cord tossed over the bar, rather than just hang the pack by its own straps.)

The foursome were cheery. One couple was from Pennsylvania, in their early twenties. This was their first backpack trip anywhere! The young woman had made the mistake of hiking in sneakers, and her feet were full of blisters. They had come down yesterday and were going out tomorrow. They didn't know about molefoams and moleskins, those miraculous adhesive-backed strips of foam and felt for use over "hotspots" and blisters. I gave her some of mine.

The other couple was in their fifties. Until we met them, Bob and I had been the oldest folks on the trail, at forty-six and thirty-seven. These two were old hands at the Hermit Trail. Every year for the last several years they had driven out from Florida to hike down and spend a few days at the little swimming hole and waterfall at Hermit Creek.

This was the first we'd heard of a pool big enough for swimming. They said it was directly below us, just a few yards upstream from where the trail from the river climbed steeply up to the campground. Since we needed water anyway, I decided to investigate. Bob didn't go. He was hurting too much. I took our two collapsible gallon jugs, clambered back down the trail to the creek, and turned left up a narrow path.

Sure enough, only a few yards away and hidden in the mesquite, there was a charming pool fed by a little waterfall. It sat in a tub in the Tapeats, no more than twenty feet across. From the boulder across from the fall, the couple from Florida had said, you could jump (not dive!) into the cold water and dog paddle. It wasn't more than six feet deep. There were tiny fishes in it. Maidenhair ferns clung to the boulders on either side of the little cascade.

No question, this was a delightful spot, and a refuge from the hot, gritty campground above. But I was just too tired to be able to enjoy it. That would come on later visits, but I had no idea then that we'd ever be back. The pool-and-fall at Hermit Creek is one of the jewels of the Grand Canyon, made so not only by its charm but by its precious rarity for the foot traveler in the Canyon.

I filled our jugs and rejoined everyone topside, treating the water with iodine tablets while we visited.

Eventually the sun moved behind the cliff that towered over us on the west, and we had shade. We said good-bye to our hosts, took our turns at the chemical latrine, and returned to our campsite. We cooked dinner on our stove (campfires are not allowed in the Canyon), ate, and cleaned up with special care for the fragile and overused environment at the campground.

We emptied our packs and left them open, so that if a skunk or ringtail cat came a-begging in the night (squirrels are diurnal), it wouldn't have to chew through them to discover there was no food. There wasn't a place where we could hang our food sacks and be confident of their inaccessibility, so we placed the food and all of our gear next to where our heads would be when we slept. (This is *not* to be done in bear country!) We leaned our cook pans and water bottles against the outside of the pile. If a critter approached, we hoped its scrabbling sounds and knocking-around of bottles and gear would wake me up. Bob sleeps soundly anywhere.

Last, we set out our army-surplus dacron sleeping bags. On my river trips, I'd learned to take the lightest possible sleeping bag in summer in the Canyon and to keep it in its stuffsack until bedtime, so as not to find the nocturnal scorpion or homeward-bound ants groping around in it when I got in. It was still too warm to be inside the bags, so we lay on top, inside the soft percale liners I had sewn for us from old sheets. They added a bit of weight to our load, but sleeping comfort is vital on the trail, and the bags' nylon covers felt clammy against the skin.

At twilight the bats came out, harbingers of night. They darted, swooped, and dived, snatching up insects. Our body clocks said it was bedtime. Bob fell asleep right away. I was too tired, too stimulated, too worried about his knee and the hike out tomorrow, too achy – too everything – to sleep. I lay for a long time, semidozing and waking. The sky was clear. The stars came out, in impossible numbers. Then the quarter moon rose and they dimmed in its light. The moon worked a witchery on the walls around us, setting them off in platinum-gray relief against the black sky. Frogs sang boisterously in the night. The waterfall below camp seemed to rebuke them with a sustained "Hushhh . . ." I lay there, enthralled. Sometime after midnight we moved into our sleeping bags, and eventually I slept.

July 4

We woke around 4 A.M. and packed up, careful to shake out our boots, clothing, and gear, in case a scorpion had found its way inside them. We hit the trail by moonlight. We wanted to have shade for as long as possible, as we'd be working harder than yesterday, hauling our packs uphill for 7 miles.

I knew I'd be able to negotiate the treacherous rocks and scree better going up than I had going down, but I didn't know how my wind would be on the steep grades. I hadn't been doing any regular cardiovascular conditioning before this trip, just hatha yoga and our mountain hiking. Bob was a soccer and basketball official in his spare time, and his wind was good; but he couldn't use his left knee.

We climbed out of the Tapeats and onto the Tonto Plateau. We passed the ranger's cabin (no one there). It was surprisingly easy to see where we were going. At our feet, the rocks seemed to hold rather than reflect a silver and yellow light. Ahead, the trail was a trough between the silhouetted bushes on either side of it. Across the Inner Gorge, the terraces and cliffs of the daytime panorama were flattened into a gigantic, sweeping gray backdrop of molars reaching eerily into space and time.

The sky began to lighten. We made it off the Tonto and into the Muav Limestone at dawn, safely in shade. The couple from Pennsylvania was behind us on the Tonto, also in shade.

Upward through the Muav and into the Redwall. Packs heavy. Hearts pounding, chests hurting, sweating. Stopping for breath, water, trail mix, and Bob's knee. The sun gaining on us. Then the view to the east through the notch in the Redwall at Cope Butte— shapes mauve, gold, slate-blue, smoky lavender, in intricate patterns of light and shadow. My mind reeled, gluttonous to take it all in and fix it forever in memory.

Breakfast atop the Redwall. Now the long trek up through the Supai Group. Still in shade, but watching the sunlight advance down the wall across from us over Hermit Gorge. Meeting occasional hikers on their way down. Plodding onward, moving slowly upward, grateful for the brief moderate stretches in the Supai. And then: a crack like a gunshot as we were approaching the end of a bay in the Supai.

We turned and looked back, just in time to see a chunk of the Supai break off the cliff in the middle of the bay and tumble down several ledges, knocking other rocks ahead of it like billiard balls. They stopped far above the trail. Then, silence.

We stood there some moments, spellbound by the event. The young couple entered the bay. They had heard the rockfall but hadn't seen it. We called across to them, "It's okay. It's over." (But could anyone be sure?) We told them what had happened. We discovered we could talk to them, a quarter of a mile across the space, in normal voices.

It was the Fourth of July, and what a display we'd just seen! We had witnessed one of the processes that had carved the Grand Canyon over the last six or more million years,[5] processes that will keep carving it until one day they will have worn it down to a broad valley, just as they twice leveled mountain ranges now missing between the Tapeats Sandstone and the Vishnu Schist.

We had to move on, and so we did. Only minutes later we met ranger Gale Burak on her way down to the ranger's cabin at Hermit. She checked our camping permit, and we told her about the rockfall. She said she'd been working seasonally at the Canyon for nearly ten years and had been hiking in it, off and on, since 1942, and in that time she had seen one small rockfall: off the top of the Coconino Sandstone on the South Kaibab Trail. She knew a few people who had seen rockfalls but said it's really unusual to see them. Later, in 1980, Gale saw a really spectacular fall.

"It happened way up in the upper Redwall, at midnight, under a full moon," she said. "I was sleeping outside the ranger station at Cottonwood Camp (7 miles up from the river on the North Kaibab Trail). The preliminary rumbling was like thunder, and it woke me up—but thunder on a cloudless full-moon night? Never. So I popped up and saw it. It was a real beauty. It made a cloud of dust like an atom bomb!"

In his 15,000 miles in 1000-plus hiking days in the Grand Canyon since 1945, Harvey Butchart has seen only a couple of small rockfalls, including a fist-sized rock that hit the trail one yard in front of him with no warning sound, in the narrows section of the North Kaibab Trail. Edward Abbey wrote in Desert Solitaire (1968) that in all his years in the canyon country he had never yet seen a rockfall, other than during floods. And Colin Fletcher heard the sound of a small stone falling a short distance only once during his two-month trek in the Grand Canyon. What incredible beginner's luck, to have seen a rockfall in the Grand Canyon!

On we went in the Supai. The sun caught up with us well before we reached Santa Maria Spring. We'd been on the trail six hours, one of us limping, the other fighting for breath all the way.

We gave ourselves a leisurely break at Santa Maria, taking and treating enough water to have two quarts each for the final pull out. Bob told me he'd had a singular moment during one of his standing pauses. I'd fallen enough behind him to be out of sight, and as he looked out at the Canyon, he had a sudden shift in perception.

"Up till then I think I had been experiencing the Canyon mostly through surface impressions," he said. "Besides, we had each other to relate to during the whole journey. But when you were out of sight, I suddenly became aware of myself, alone, in relation to the Canyon.

"It was one of those last-man-on-earth sensations, right out of the 'Twilight Zone,' where the camera pulls up and away, leaving the character standing in the immensity of his aloneness, alone in the immensity of his surroundings. Those incredible distances, colors, and textures had been here for so long, I thought, only seen by mankind in the past brief few thousand years, and by me for the first time now, a split instant in the Canyon's existence. I didn't feel insignificant, just fortunate to be experiencing it.

"When you pulled into view around a bend in the trail, I shifted from what had felt like a higher plane of awareness back to the reality of heat, trail dust, and aching muscles. And our companionship."

Resuming. Up into Hermit Basin and the steep, rutted path up the Hermit Shale to the foot of the Coconino Sandstone. Stopping to drink, to nibble, to catch breath, ease pain, wipe away sweat. Then up and up and up the Coconino. Stopping in swatches of shade offered by trees. My eyes chanced to fall on a trailside boulder with a flat top. On it, a human acting in an obviously official capacity had long ago stenciled in neat black letters, partially erased by weathering over the decades:

800 FEET
BELOW RIM.[6]

I didn't know whether to rejoice or to cry.

Up the relentless switchbacks of the Toroweap Formation and the Kaibab Limestone. A light breeze and intermittent shade helped some, but I was wishing I was anyplace but on this trail. Ruefully I admitted to myself that I was not in proper condition for hiking in the Grand Canyon. I needed to learn how to walk downhill on rubble and scree, and I needed to be in aerobic condition for the uphill grades.

Finally it was over. We were out, back on the rim. We straggled up the service road and back to the rim at Hermits Rest. We looked out again at Hermit Gorge and down at the Tonto Plateau. We actually had been down on that sunseared, rolling platform. From here it looked gray and featureless, but we knew otherwise. We had been there, towering over the blackbrush like Gulliver in a Lilliputian forest. We had been down inside that brooding black wrinkle where there were gemlike falls and pools and flowers and grasses and even little fishes—things you couldn't guess existed down there when you stood on the rim. We had cooled our feet in the river, beside one of the most exciting rapids in the world, deep inside rocks formed before there was any life on earth. And we had witnessed an event of Canyon-making-and-destroying that few people have ever seen.

We began to feel elated at our success, and to feel grateful. We had *experienced* the Grand Canyon, not just looked at it from the rim. Even though, as beginners here, we had been occupied by the minute-to-minute urgencies of our physical limitations, the Canyon's elemental power and beauty had not been lost on us. We had had direct contact with it.

We knew we'd be back, on the dory trip next year. We didn't know then that we'd also be back on foot, many times. We would discover on later trips that although we would always be beset by the physical demands of the trail, we would also gain greatly in our ability to see and hear and smell and feel—and to just BE in the Canyon.

I took our trash sack from my pack and dropped it into a nearby bin. Then we caught the shuttle back to the Village, drove to the BRO to check in, and went to our motel. Tomorrow we would start for home.

Notes

1. Apostrophes are deleted on possessive-named features on topographic maps, and these are the accepted spellings for text as well.

2. This sign has since been removed and replaced by standard GCNP trail signage. Also, the BRO used to be at the visitors center but since has been moved to a separate building across the South Entrance Road from the visitors center.

3. Figures on the time spans in the Great Unconformity vary. These are from Larry Stevens's *The Colorado River in Grand Canyon: A Guide* (Red Lake Books, Flagstaff, Arizona, 1983, pp. 9–10).

4. Thickness ranges are given in the geologic chart in appendix A.

5. Estimates of the Canyon's age—i.e., the carving by the river and the incision of its side canyons by gravity, weathering, and erosion—vary up to 25 million years. Stephen Whitney, author of *A Field Guide to the Grand Canyon* (Quill, New York, 1982, p. 242), narrows it down to 2.6 to 10 million years. In his *An Introduction to Grand Canyon Geology* (Grand Canyon Natural History Association, 1980, p. 37), Michael Collier says the Colorado River has been eroding the Canyon for 6 million years. Geologist and Grand Canyon trail guide Jim R. Ohlman supports the 6-million-year estimate.

6. It definitely was not graffiti, nor was it a United States Geological Survey (USGS) benchmark. The "sign" was placed so that a rider on a mule would easily have seen it. No one I talked to at the park service knew about it, but when I described it to Louise M. Hinchliffe, librarian at the Grand Canyon from 1951 to 1985, she speculated it may have been painted on the rock by one of the Santa Fe Railroad's trail builders or its mule guides. If so, there may be or may have been other such markers along the trail.

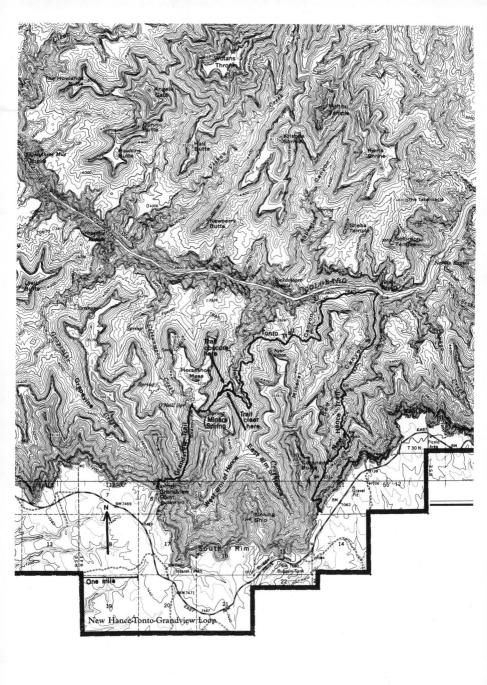

New Hance-Tonto-Grandview Loop

CHAPTER 2

New Hance-Tonto-Grandview Loop
September 1981

The river trip in 1980 was all it had been in 1978 — more, because Bob was with me. We were able to relax and plug into the river's time, and with it to gradually accept, even if we couldn't grasp, the enormous spans of time in the rocks. The river carried us downward into them, beginning with the exposure of the Kaibab Limestone just below Lees Ferry, mile 0, and ending at the Grand Wash Cliffs at mile 277.

We had a spectacular ride in Hermit Rapids. At the bottom, we looked at the shore where we had stood looking back only a year before, and we felt a fullness in knowing we had made the difficult but rewarding passage down to it on foot.

No sooner were we home than I was scheming to take us back to the Canyon. At first I had in mind a combined trip. We'd hike down the New Hance Trail to Hance Rapids at mile 77, meet the dories and stay with them a week, then hike out from Havasu, mile 157. But the more I thought about the New Hance Trail, the more interested I became in making the hike for its own sake and to extend it into a loop with the Tonto and Grandview trails.

Never mind that my guidebooks warned that the New Hance was tough and in places hard to follow. We were ready to try it. We were confident this hike would go more smoothly than the Hermit had. For one thing, we knew better what to expect. For another, I was in better condition. I'd been jogging regularly, teaching yoga, and had backpacked ten days in Utah's Canyonlands

National Park on a Colorado Outward Bound School women's course. There I'd gained greater confidence and skill on rocks.

Our plan was to hike the New Hance Trail 7-or-so miles and 4400 vertical feet to the river, the only reliable water source, and to camp at Hance Rapids. The second day we'd take the Tonto Trail 8 miles west to Horseshoe Mesa, getting water at Miners Spring and camping on the mesa. The third day we'd hike the Grandview Trail 3 miles and 2600 feet back up to the rim.

We'd go in early September. It would still be hot, with temperatures near 100 degrees on the Tonto Plateau. There also was a chance of rain. September is on the tag end of the so-called monsoon season at the Grand Canyon (usually afternoon thundershowers, mid-July to mid-September). Almost an inch of rain can fall in the Inner Gorge in September. We'd take our tent, just in case.

The Hance-Grandview district is rich in recent history. "Captain" John Hance was a prospector and yarn spinner who came to the Grand Canyon in 1883 and became its first white settler. He improved a prehistoric Indian route down the east arm of what later became known as Hance Canyon, and he worked his asbestos mines high on the steep slope across the river from Mineral Canyon and around the corner up Asbestos Canyon. From Hance Rapids you can see the tailings below one of the tunnels. Hance rowed across the river above Hance Rapids at low water, after spring runoff, and had a trail leading up to the mines.

Hance soon found a richer lode—tourism. In 1884, he led the Edward Everett Ayer family to the bottom of the Canyon, thus becoming the first tour guide in the Grand Canyon, and Mrs. Ayer became the first white woman to make the descent on foot. Ayer Point to the east of Hance Canyon is named for the Ayers. Hance continued to guide tourists, putting them up at his cabin on the rim and leading them down his trail on foot, horse, or mule, entertaining them with tall tales. He also raised vegetables and continued to mine his asbestos claims.

In 1894, rockslides knocked out portions of his trail, and rather than rebuild it, he built a new one down Red Canyon, to the east. He led his guests down it on mules to accommodations at Hance Rapids. From there he took them west on the Tonto Trail to Horseshoe Mesa, where they stayed at the miners' cabins, and back to the rim at Grand View Point. He could complete this loop because the Tonto Trail already existed as a prehistoric Indian route and because Pete Berry had built a trail from Horseshoe Mesa to Grand View Point along another prehistoric Indian route.

Berry was a miner who had worked his way west to Flagstaff, Arizona. In 1890 he laid claim to the Last Chance copper mine high in the Redwall on the east side of Horseshoe Mesa. He claimed a mill site on the rim and built his trail, known initially as the Berry Trail and later as the Grandview Trail (the spelling changed somewhere along the way), in 1892.

Berry and the other miners of Horseshoe Mesa received a lot of visitors at their mines, cabins, and cookhouse and, like John Hance, Berry came to see them as a valuable source of income. He expanded his cabin on the rim into a two-story log structure called the Grand View Hotel, which he opened in 1897. Even though the ore at the Last Chance mine was of good quality, it was not as profitable as tourism.

Tourism at Hance and Grand View thrived until the Santa Fe Railroad began its branch-line service from Williams, Arizona to the present Grand Canyon Village area in 1901. As tourism developed there at the Bright Angel trailhead, it waned for Berry and Hance.

Berry sold the Last Chance mine in 1901 but hung onto his hotel, serving meals to day trippers from the Village until 1908. Then it closed. Only the outlines of the hotel's foundations remain. The bottom fell out of the copper market, and mining on Horseshoe Mesa died by 1908, but relics of its structures and the mines in the Redwall still exist.

Hance sold his ranch and trail in 1895 but stayed on there, in 1897 claiming yet another first: he became the first postmaster on the rim, when the post office of Tourist, Arizona was established at Hance Ranch. In 1907, a new owner of Hance Ranch, Martin Buggeln (pronounced "*Bug*-len"), built a small, two-story hotel adjoining the ranch. Hance sold his mines and managed them for their eastern owners until 1904.

Eventually, John Hance ended up at Grand Canyon Village, where the Fred Harvey Company hired him as a "colorful character" to greet and amuse tourists with his humorous yarns at Bright Angel Lodge.

Like the Grand View Hotel, the Hance Ranch and the Buggeln Hotel structures no longer exist.

There has been considerable confusion about the names of the trails John Hance built. In addition, the rapids named after him isn't at the mouth of Hance Canyon, where it logically ought to be, but at the mouth of Red Canyon. All can be explained.

In 1869, Major John Wesley Powell led the first expedition on the Colorado River through the Grand Canyon. He named the rapids at the mouth of what later came to be called Hance Canyon "Sockdolager." It was a boxing colloquialism of Powell's day meaning "knockdown blow." Thus, the rapids later named after John Hance was the one at Red Canyon.

Hance most likely did not name his trail in Hance Canyon after himself. The trail was known simply as the Old Trail. Only parts of this route remain. It is not shown on the 1962 topographic map, and it is considered to be extremely hazardous even for experienced Grand Canyon hikers.

The trail down Red Canyon is usually called the New Hance Trail. Since Hance's first trail didn't bear his name, "New" is actually a misnomer. The topographic map shows this trail and calls it the Hance Trail. The park service's Backcountry Trip Planner map, which is included in the BRO's Trip Planning Packet, calls it the New Hance Trail. Another NPS map, the GCNP Backcountry Use Area Map, dated 1982, shows it as the Red Canyon Trail. Harvey Butchart suggests, "All confusion would be avoided by calling it the Red Canyon Trail," but concedes that he would be content to see the trail continue to have all three names, especially to honor its builder. For consistency with park service trail signage, I call it the New Hance Trail, misnomer and all.

When Bob and I arrived at the Grand Canyon, we headed for Moran Point to try to see what we could of the New Hance Trail, which, even with binoculars, was nothing. The Thybony *Guide to Hiking the Inner Canyon* and Harvey Butchart's *Grand Canyon Treks* cautioned that the trail is obscure in places. We looked at one another wonderingly.

Next, we located the trailhead. In 1981, it was still vague, but by 1984 increased hiker use had led the park service to make it easily found.

At a dip in the East Rim Drive just over 1 mile southwest of the turn-in to Moran Point or 4.8 miles east of the Grandview Point turn-in, there is a white-gravel widening of the shoulder of the road, with three "No Parking Tow Away" signs. Hikers must not park there! A row of boulders blocks a disused service road, which leads directly to the trailhead, petering out to trail width just before it gets there. It's about a four-minute walk. The bulletin board sign just before you reach the wood trailhead sign says it's 6.6 miles to the river. The Thybony guide says it's 8. It's probably about 7, but even experienced hikers agree it feels more like 9. From the trailhead we could see only the first couple of switchbacks in the trees and Coronado Butte to the northwest.

We had better luck at Grandview Point. With binoculars we could see people on the Grandview Trail, and we'd been told it was popular with day hikers and is easily followed. Reassured, we went to the BRO for our permit. As we had for the Hermit, and as we always would, we elected to check in at the end of the trip for safety's sake. Then we went to our lodging and called the Fred Harvey Taxi Service to arrange for transportation the next day.

September 5

At 6:30 A.M. we pulled up to the taxi office. As promised, the driver was there. He followed us to Grandview Point, 8.75 miles out the East Rim Drive from its junction with the South Entrance Road. We parked there, loaded our packs into the van, and rode to the turn-in for the New Hance trailhead. We put on our packs and walked to the trailhead, pausing briefly to recheck the map and my outline of the descriptions in Butchart and Thybony.

We stepped onto the trail in high spirits, even though the sky was lightly overcast.

If one word could sum up the descent of the New Hance Trail, I would choose "Yiii. . . ." Bob's choice would be "Argh." The trail takes hikers on a treacherously steep, rocky, scree-y, slippy-slidy careen to the floor of Red Canyon. In spite of this, I moved with less trepidation than I had on the Hermit Trail two years before. My physical preparations paid off. But even Bob was less than his usual serene self on the New Hance Trail.

The trail began in a ravine on the east side of the head of the west arm of Red Canyon. It headed north down the wooded, cream-and-buff-colored Kaibab, Toroweap, and Coconino formations in steep, rubbly switchbacks. Occasional animal droppings reminded us we weren't alone. While we were still in the Kaibab Limestone,

we watched two ravens soaring on thermals, croaking and perform-
ing the aerial acrobatics for which these raucous birds are known.
To me, they were mimicking our own high spirits. But if I'd believed
in omens, I'd have said they were laughing at these fool humans.

As we descended, we glanced out at the changing scene and
back up and thought, "Have we really come that far already?" Cairns
marked the route in places, mostly to help hikers see the trail coming
up, we supposed.

We had breakfast in the Coconino Sandstone, amid boulders
and large junipers. We looked out across the Inner Gorge at Vishnu
Temple, with Rama Shrine in front and to the right of it. Then,
back on foot. More switchbacks, more cairns. Bob favored the term
"duck" for the small piles of rocks, considering "cairns" to be larger
mounds of rocks. Technically, a duck is a trail marker of only two
rocks, a cairn anything larger. Still, there were so many markers
on the trail, Bob called it a "duck walk." "Cairn walk" just didn't
have the right ring.

The cairns had probably all been put along the trail by over-
zealous hikers. The park service discourages cairn-building by hikers
in the park. It puts up signs and markers on the maintained trails
only as "justified for visitor safety," making them only as obvious
as necessary.[1] This is to preserve the wilderness character of the
traveler's experience.

In any case, there is an etiquette about cairn-building that can
be summed up thus: (1) Build a marker only if it's really needed,
not merely to decorate a clearly defined trail, no matter how insistent
your duck-urge may be. (2) Make sure it is marking the correct trail.
If it isn't, take it and anyone else's mistakes down. (3) Don't put
markers on cross-country routes or routes that are being abandoned
for a specific reason. (4) Make your marker small, only just large
enough to be clearly recognized as a trail marker.

Our trail turned west briefly in the red Hermit Shale. Then it
descended north-northeast down through the blocky, ledgy,
red-brown Supai Group, following a major drainage on the east
flank of Coronado Butte. The descent was long, and the trail was
a mess of rubble and scree. It crossed and re-crossed the drainage
many times, staying sometimes high, sometimes low, until at last
it reached the top of the Redwall. According to the map, this drain-

age eventually heads into Red Canyon, but the trail didn't stay in it. Instead, it circled northeasterly along the top of the Redwall, now near the edge, now back from it, crossing many side drainages that were jumbled with Supai slides. The trail to the Redwall break was obvious, but it was rough and up-and-down, sometimes steeply so. It went on and on, and it always gave dramatic views of the Redwall cliff just across to the west.

At last we reached the break on the east side of a drainage that comes in northwest of Moran Point. We dropped over the edge of the Redwall, and although the descent wasn't very exposed, it was treacherous. We spilled down not switchbacks, but corkscrews. It was so precipitous it seemed more like a barely controlled slide. The trail was very rough—broken, slippery. We took the descent in baby steps, seeking anchor rocks to break or prevent a skid. Our thighs were quivering with strain. Three-quarters of a century after John Hance left his ranch for good, nature had almost reclaimed the trail he had brought guests down on mules.

The trail in the Redwall stayed on the east side of the drainage, and so did the passage through the Muav Limestone and the Bright Angel Shale, both of which moderated somewhat to a steep traverse across a rolling slope out along a ridge. Juniper trees were scattered on the slope, existing here well below their usual range. Now we could see, in lower Red Canyon, the vivid red-orange to rust-red (some would say vermilion) slanting beds of the Hakatai Shale, from which Red Canyon gets its name. The Hakatai is one of the members of the Grand Canyon Supergroup exposed in this part of the Grand Canyon.

Soon we entered the Hakatai (the Tapeats Sandstone should have been below the Bright Angel Shale but it was missing here). The descent began on the east side of Red Canyon and was a steep traverse around a ridge, along a rutted, gravelly, rust-red slope. Fortunately, the shaley gravel wasn't slippery, but the descent was so relentlessly steep that our thighs, knees, and calves ached with the strain of constant braking. The trail was clear and stayed in the Hakatai, crossing a tributary from the southeast and remaining on the east wall of Red Canyon until it finally reached the canyon floor, still in the Hakatai, in the last mile and a half before the river.

In the creekbed, just above the intersection of the trail with the canyon floor, there was a cottonwood tree. Here, we'd been told, there may be seasonal water flowing. There was, but rather than load up again, we decided to wait till the river.

The walk down the bed was the first real relief to our legs since we'd begun, but even the bed descended steadily. We glanced up at the sky, still a light gray overcast. No rain around the Red Canyon drainage. That was reassuring, as this bed could channel an angry, roaring, muscular brute of a flood. Hance Rapids was a testimonial to that.

About a mile down the bed we came to the first of several low, dry falls. Rather than scramble down them, we looked around, as we'd learned to do when things looked a little vague. Sure enough, cairns led to bypasses on the right and on the left, up in the mesquite and brittlebushes on the banks. We followed the bypasses around the falls and back into the bed. And now we could hear Hance Rapids and see Solomon Temple towering dead ahead.

So far today there'd been few scenic flights overhead to break the Canyon's deep quiet. We'd met no hikers coming up the trail. We didn't know if there were others coming down, and we liked having this raw and starkly beautiful corner of the Canyon to ourselves.

We continued our slow advance and reached the rapids just after 1 P.M. Our feet were hot and our legs ached. The New Hance Trail had earned its reputation as a beast in a beautiful setting. But now we had the whole afternoon to be at leisure. How different from our Hermit trek two years before!

My heart sank at the first view of Hance Rapids. The water was very low. The three times I'd ridden through Hance, it was big, wild, and tricky, a churning froth hiding boat-bruising boulders. Today it was a garden of exposed rocks. Then I remembered: this was Labor Day Weekend. Phoenix and other cities dependent on regional power sources, including Glen Canyon Dam, 92 miles upriver, wouldn't be using as much electricity in their commercial buildings as on weekdays. The result: less water released into the Canyon.

Three years from now I'd laugh out loud reading an anecdote about Hance Rapids in a letter from Harvey Butchart. He told how bulldozers were brought to Phantom Ranch for the construction of its sewage disposal plant at the mouth of Bright Angel Creek, mile 87.5. "They were floated down from Lees Ferry on the largest rafts," he wrote. "They say the operator of one of the backhoes was in the driver's seat as they came through Hance and Sockdolager, blowing the horn and working the windshield wiper. The machines were dismantled after construction ended and brought to the rim by helicopter."

Hance Rapids offered no such amusement today.

We camped on a dune above the west side of the creek, where we'd be high and dry in case it rained and Red Canyon flash flooded. We set up our tent under questionable skies and went to the river for water.

The river was running reddish brown, carrying a sediment load from rains and flash floods in side canyons upstream. Fortunately, having carried five quarts each, Bob and I had enough drinking water to last through dinner. We'd have plenty of time to let the river water settle in our collapsible jugs before we decanted it into our bottles and treated it with iodine tablets.

We went about this and other camp chores. Bob had brought his 35mm camera with the automatic timer, and we took some photos, including one of us at our tent in front of the dark red slope of Hakatai Shale across the emasculated river. Atop the Hakatai rested the massive purple-brown cliff of the Shinumo Quartzite, another member of the Grand Canyon Supergroup. The tailings and entrance to one of John Hance's asbestos mines were visible high on the slope far downriver. There was no Vishnu Schist here, but we could see it emerge just downstream from Hance's mine.

We spent the afternoon relaxing. We wondered if any river parties would come (none did) and if they'd be able to run the rapids at such low water. Late in the afternoon another hiking party came down and camped on the other side of the creek. They probably relished being alone in this part of the Canyon, as we did, so we never spoke.

The sky lowered and there were some sprinkles. Then they stopped, and the sky upriver cleared to a cobalt blue. Downstream it held storm clouds. For a short time in the late afternoon the sun shot through the clouds and cast a bronze light on a low peak framed between the upstream walls. A later check of our map showed it to be an unnamed peak off the west arm of Escalante Butte. Behind it and to its right we could see the cylindrical stone Watchtower on the South Rim at Desert View, the east entrance to Grand Canyon National Park.

It rained all night, a quiet, steady rain. There was no thunder or lightning. We slept well, occasionally waking and luxuriating in the gentle wet sounds around us, the rumble of the rapids, and the dry comfort inside the tent.

September 6

It really was the most accommodating of weather. Our beautiful night rains ended before morning. Rivulets of rusty sludge braided the mouth of Red Canyon, trickling down to the river named for the red-brown loads it carried—the Colorado. Before Glen Canyon Dam upstream closed it off in 1963, the Colorado River transported an average of 500,000 tons of silt, pebbles, and boulders past the gauging station at Bright Angel Creek every day, and many times that in peak runoff years. This was the abrasive edge that carried away all the rocks in the Grand Canyon over six million years. Since the dam was built, the sediment load from the river's bed, banks, and side drainages has been cut by a good four-fifths. The river drops its sediments in Lake Powell above the dam and then is released through penstocks at the toe of the dam. It runs cold and green, except when rain or runoff in tributary drainages pushes their loads into it.

We were able to get the tent pretty well dried out in time to still get an early start. We were facing 8 miles on the Tonto Plateau, and we knew all too well how hot it would be by late morning if the sun came out. (Great hiker's luck: the weather would accommodate us all day. It stayed overcast but never rained, clearing when we arrived in camp.)

Red Canyon at mile 77 marks the beginning of the Tonto Trail, a mostly waterless cross-canyon route that takes 85 to 95 foot miles,[2] following side canyons, to cover only 37 river miles, ending at Garnet Canyon downstream at mile 114. The cairn-marked Escalante Route goes upriver from Hance Rapids to Tanner Rapids, mile 68.5, and the Beamer Trail extends from there to the confluence of the Little Colorado River at mile 62, but these routes aren't considered part of the Tonto Trail, since the Tonto Plateau as such does not exist upstream from Red Canyon. Neither the Escalante nor the Beamer is shown on the 1962 topo map, but they are shown on the BRO's Backcountry Trip Planner map.

Gale Burak, the ranger Bob and I met on the Hermit Trail after the rockfall in the Supai, has done extensive historical research on the trails in the Grand Canyon. She told us how the Tonto Trail evolved:

"Like Topsy, it just grew. From the ruins of bivouacs, mescal pits, and artifacts along the length of the Tonto and in the vicinity of the plateau, it seems most evident that it was used as a thoroughfare by the peoples who inhabited the Canyon—from the split-twig figurine makers of the Desert Culture some 3000 to 5000 years ago, to the Pueblo Anasazi of the Kayenta Culture from about 1050 to 1150 A.D., to the more recent Havasupais and Paiutes. The animals used it, too, of course, but the browsers (those large enough to make a trail impact) are wanderers. They make many trails, one leading into five others, back and forth across the slopes, here and there where there's a good bush or wallow-dust hollow. The first whites, the miners, followed the old stretches of Indian trails, again as an easier way of getting east and west than to have to ascend to the rim, go along it, and then descend again. If Pete Berry wanted to visit the Camerons (at Indian Gardens and the Bright Angel trailhead) or even Bill Bass (Bass Canyon is at mile 108), that'd be the way he'd go."

The Tonto Trail stays on the Tonto Plateau except when it crosses major side canyons, where it dips into the older underlying rock. It's seldom flat. It's usually climbing up or easing down a slope. The trail is obscure in places, especially west of Slate Creek, mile 98. By scanning ahead you can usually see it (except, again, west of Slate). Sometimes animal trails confuse the main route. Cairns mark it in some of these places and at drainage crossings. As you approach a drainage, it's advisable to spot where the trail continues on the far side before crossing. If you don't, you can end up retracing your steps to scan ahead anyway. Because it must follow side canyons, the Tonto tends to stay back from the river, only occasionally nearing the verge of the Inner Gorge or even giving a view of the river.

Bob and I set out west along the dune we'd camped on, and there was the trail with, sure enough, a cairn where it swung upward.

(You can also strike west along the upper dune and meet the trail, which is obvious from there.) The trail made a rapid, rocky rise up and across grassy talus, between boulders and across slides, heading toward Mineral Canyon. The trail was sometimes steep, and it paralleled the river for a long time. Then it turned and climbed up and away from the river and passed briefly through a field of elephant-sized boulders and desert brush. The gravelly, rust-red Hakatai Shale was once again underfoot and remained so as the trail climbed steadily and often steeply. It crossed Mineral Canyon and continued climbing up through the Tapeats Sandstone, until it rounded Ayer Point. On the far side of Ayer Point, the trail finally leveled out on top of the Tapeats—on the *real* Tonto Plateau, complete with blackbrush, at long last.

And now the brooding black west wall of Hance Canyon came into view. Hance Canyon was immense. Below the flake-pastry of the Tapeats Sandstone, its walls of Vishnu Schist glowered, thrusting darkly up from the floor a thousand feet below. The trail stayed clear and essentially smooth and level as we moved toward the head of the canyon.

We looked back to the north. A tiny swatch of river was visible through the notch of Hance Canyon, and we had a dramatic view of Vishnu Temple directly above it, flanked by Rama Shrine on the east and Krishna Shrine on the west. Behind and farther west was Wotans Throne. These features dominated the scenery in this part of the Canyon. At 7529 feet, Vishnu Temple towered majestically more than a thousand feet above Rama and Krishna, tapering to a peak of Kaibab Limestone. Wotan was a wooded mesa capped by Kaibab Limestone.

Vishnu Temple rose in a gigantic river-to-peak stacking of the strata. On top of the Vishnu Schist of the Inner Gorge were three members of the Grand Canyon Supergroup: first, the ledgy gray cliff of the Bass Limestone; above it, the orange-and-red Hakatai Shale; then, the purple-brown cliff of the Shinumo Quartzite. The Tapeats Sandstone should have rested on top of the Shinumo, but it was missing there. The Great Unconformity occurred at the seam where the Bright Angel Shale (Tonto Plateau) rested on the Shinumo. Above the Tonto was the usual layering leading to the Kaibab peak of Vishnu Temple. It was a stupendous staircase, normally resonant in color, flattened today in the light gray overcast.

At the Tonto Trail's intersection with Hance Canyon, we descended briefly into the Hance drainage, still high in the Tapeats. We found an inviting, shady nook in the Tapeats against the east wall and ate lunch there, appreciating the visual shift from the terrible and grand to the friendly and small. We shared our lunchroom with desert shrubs and a collared lizard.

Onward, across the creekbed—abundant vegetation and seasonal water flowing there—past a couple of campsites on the west, and then a brief climb back out onto the Tonto Plateau. The sky was beginning to clear. In less than a half mile, we came to a wash and the junction with the trail to Horseshoe Mesa. Ahead, the Tonto Trail continued out Hance Canyon and around the mesa. To the left, it headed southwest up the wash. We turned left.

And now came twenty minutes of confusion and concern. As we climbed up and along the steep west side of the wash, the trail became faint and then disappeared. We took a wrong turn uphill and had to retrace our steps. Bob walked into a prickly pear cactus and got a shinful of spines and glochids, the tiny barbed bristles at the base of the spines that detach easily from the plant. I tweezed them out. "Nothing like a shinful of cactus to focus your attention," Bob said.

I was growing worried. I knew we weren't lost, but I was frustrated. We knew our route was up the west side of the wash and that Miners Spring (shown only as "Spring" on the topo map) was on the east side of the head of the wash. *But where was the trail?*

We picked our way across the rippling of small ridges and dips on the steep slope, along an indistinct trace, and suddenly we were back on real trail again. I bawled with relief.

In November 1984, Bob day hiked our loop solo, an eighteen-mile feat worthy of Harvey Butchart and one which is not to be attempted except by the most athletic, endurance-proven and experienced Grand Canyon hikers. Bob made these notes from the crossing of Hance Canyon to the resumption of trail in the wash:

> Shortly after entering Hance I go too far down into the camping area. Trails lead from there down Hance Canyon. That's not the way. Need to go up, not down. Retrace, find Tonto Trail once again and resume. Reach wash. Now a tall cairn marks junction with trail to Horseshoe Mesa. In the middle of the wash, another tall cairn beckons up the wash. *This is not the way we came in 1981.*

Worry time here. No trail to be seen. Ducks, though. Follow them up wash over some rocks and come to a thickness of boulders and vegetation. Look around, see ducks leading steeply up a narrow ridge on the west wall. Follow them on very faint trail. Scan around where to go next. See duck pointing me across a shallow dip on my left and can barely make out a trace leading to it. Take the trace across dip, past duck and up onto next ridge-let. Suddenly, strong, clear trail again. This must be where it resumed in 1981. How did we find our way to it then?

In November 1985, the route was finally clear—but for who knows how much longer? We backpacked the loop again, and this time we came upon a cairn-marked fork on the Tonto Trail only about a quarter of a mile from the intersection of the Tonto Trail with Hance Canyon. Bob decided to try to repeat his 1984 route and stayed low. I went left at the fork on a clear, easy trail that led another quarter of a mile over a ridge and down into the east side of the wash. (Later, from above, I saw still another clear trail over that ridge that roughly paralleled my trail.) Bob stayed in view below me as he came directly up the wash, then began wandering around on the west side. The cairns were changed, he said, and he proceeded to have a reprise of our 1981 experience, complete with the collision with a cactus and wanderings that led nowhere. My clear trail on the east side, meanwhile, took me down into the wash, crossed it, and brought me directly onto the resumption of clear trail on the west side. Bob walked across his trackless slope and rejoined me.

All of this is a reminder that the trails in the Grand Canyon change over time, often are different from how they're shown on the topo maps, and also may become confused with the search-tracks of previous hikers.

Bob and I trudged on, grateful to be on a trail again. It was steep, mind-numbingly steep, climbing toward the head of the wash. The trail remained clear. It stayed on the west flank of the eroded slope of Bright Angel Shale and Muav Limestone and, according to the map, climbed nearly 700 feet in the half mile or so to the junction with the short trail to Miners Spring. We could see in the distance the greenery at the spring.

A cairn marked the fork to the trail to Miners Spring, off to the left. We reached the spring in two minutes. It was delicious and cool, tucked into a shady niche at the base of the Redwall. In the late 1800s, the miners of Horseshoe Mesa carved its shallow basin, and mule trains brought water 3000 feet and 3.5 miles up to the rim to supply the Grand View Hotel and miners' settlement.

The spring was overhung by a ledge of limestone draped with grasses and ferns. Redbud trees grew around it and framed the view outward, creating a perfectly balanced composition: On the left, the Redwall cliff of Horseshoe Mesa. On the right, partially screened by redbuds, the steeply sloping terrace of the east wall. Center, in vibrant colors now that the clouds were breaking up, Krishna, Vishnu, and Rama. Background to their left, the distant, wooded cliffs of the North Rim. And above it all, unifying it, a sky becoming dream-blue with fleecy white clouds.

While we rested, we took and treated a gallon of water each, more than enough for the rest of the day and the short haul out the next. Then we returned to the main trail and started up the Redwall on narrow, rocky, steep switchbacks. We passed a mine entrance, with relics outside it telling quietly of the noisy, backbreak-

Krishna, Vishnu, and Rama, seen from Miners Spring

Mine entrance in Redwall, east side of Horseshoe Mesa

ing work of the late 1800s. Small pieces of blue-green copper ore were scattered at the site. We investigated only the entry – the tunnels and shafts the mines contain are unstable. Above the mine, the trail became more and more difficult – narrower, rougher, steeper, and exposed. Once or twice our metal pack frames bumped and scraped against the cliff wall, jostling our balance under the shifting loads. We agreed we would not want to come *down* this trail, with or without packs on. The very top was the most treacherous. We skirted under a low overhang and had to make one unpleasant scramble.

As we climbed the Redwall, I tried to ignore my fright by picturing in my mind the trains of eight or ten mules, each animal carrying 200 pounds of ore, making one and a half round trips to the rim each day. (Of course, the trail was broad and maintained back then, which was difficult to imagine.) I listened for the sounds that rang out into the Canyon's stillness in those days before airplanes: the clank and crunch of picks and shovels into rock; the thunder of explosives reverberating off the walls; the creak and groan of the mule-operated hoist that brought the ore to the surface; the animal's labored breathing; the heavy clatter of the trolley on the narrow gauge track out to the dump; and the voices of the miners, grunting and talking to themselves in the mines, telling raucous and no doubt raunchy stories and sharing dreams in their mess hall and cabins just south of Horseshoe Mesa Butte. And I thought about those who came down the route of the Grandview Trail for centuries before the miners, to get the ore to use for paint–Hopi Indians, who lived east of the Canyon and traded with the Havasupais to the west.

All silent now. And all of it–mines, pieces of ore, artifacts, remnant structures–all of it, like the 2000 or more prehistoric Indian ruins in the Canyon, protected by federal and state laws. Camping is prohibited at these sites, and nothing may be removed or even moved, as context–association–is important in understanding the meaning of any artifact. It's also important not to lean against ruins, as they can, and do, collapse.

The miners left another legacy, one that has had a greater impact on Canyon ecology than their mines ever did: burros.

The Grand Canyon was full of prospectors in the late 1800s. They came with horses, mules, and burros or on foot, and they filed hundreds of claims. The burro was a particularly hardy pack animal for the Canyon. A small donkey, native not to America but to North Africa, the burro could subsist on almost any sort of vegetation and move on terrain too difficult for mules or horses. Some prospectors released their burros to feed and multiply, possibly losing some to the wilderness. Others left their burros when they quit their claims.

The wild burros thrived, reducing forage for other animals, hastening erosion, and fouling water sources. By 1924, it was recognized that the burros were damaging Canyon resources, and the National Park Service destroyed 2800 of them between 1924 and 1969, to the dismay and outrage of animal lovers. Several hundred burros remained, however, and by 1980 the park service was planning to get rid of them, again by the most cost-effective means– shooting them. Hard-pressed for funds for the park, the NPS said live removal would cost about $1400 per animal and take months, whereas shooting them would cost only $30,000 and take only three weeks.

Sensitive to public outcry, the NPS offered to let the public try to remove the burros alive, and writer Cleveland Amory's Fund for Animals (FFA) became the principal organization involved. Between July 1980 and August 1981, volunteers with FFA rounded up and airlifted out 572 burros, trucking them to the fund's rescue ranch in Texas for eventual adoption by private parties. The operation cost the fund $500,000. Amory found the burros sociable, interesting, and affectionate and said they adjusted quickly to domestic life.

On our river trip in 1980, Bob and I had seen a family of burros on the north side of the river below mile 200. They were a handsome silver gray and appeared sleek and well fed. It was a fleeting contact, but I still wondered where they were now.

We emerged onto the neck of Horseshoe Mesa and into a world of sunlight and space. The Canyon opened all around us. The mesa was cloaked in greens and golds. We found a previously used campsite on the neck (the park service later established designated sites and a toilet along the east edge of the mesa) and went about camp chores. Two day hikers came by, on their way back to the rim from exploring the mesa. We talked awhile, and after they left we discovered they'd left pop cans and loose lunch wrappers at a small boulder nearby. It made us sad and angry that people who would make the effort to explore a challenging wild environment would not leave it as clean as they found it. We crushed their cans and stuffed them and the wrappers into our trash sack.

Near sunset the west wall of Coronado Butte glowed rose, yellow, and coral beneath purple clouds fringed in pink and platinum. We used the tent that night, but the rains didn't return. Through the slanting doorway, we could see a quarter moon and occasional wisps of clouds.

September 7

It was a mellow night on the mesa, and morning came with golden promise. Our hike was going to be short and it wasn't hot, so we were in no hurry to leave. We explored, took pictures, checked the map.

We struck out after midmorning, full of anticipation, and the Grandview Trail did not let us down. In every conceivable way it fulfilled the morning's promise. The trail was steep but seldom exposed, except for the last few switchbacks at the top, where once again our packs scraped against the wall. It offered views that were generous, rich, luminous, and varied. We took our time and stopped frequently. We turned around in order to see what hikers descending the Grandview would see and were equally delighted.

The trail went south from Horseshoe Mesa on top of the Redwall and was always in pinyon-juniper woodland with its associates: the broomlike Mormon tea; mountain mahogany; grasses and late-blooming wildflowers; pale hoptree, with its skunklike, citrusy aroma that's supposed to keep livestock from browsing it; and Utah serviceberry, an important browse for deer and a source of food for both birds and Indians.

Abundant along the trail was the Utah agave, my favorite Grand Canyon plant. Also called mescal,[3] maguey, or century plant, the agave has a poignance: it blooms only once, at the end of a fifteen-to-twenty-five-year life, and then it dies. From the center of its rosette of daggerlike leaves it sends up a flower stalk three to fourteen feet high, with myriad bell-shaped yellow flowers in clusters on the upper two-thirds of the stalk. The Indians roasted the roots and shoots of the agave in "mescal pits," circular pits lined with hot rocks, twenty feet or more across. Mescal pits are the most common archaeological remains in the Grand Canyon. The agave is especially spectacular when it's in bloom and is backlit. It's found rim to river, and that's another reason I'm so fond of it. It's like a sentinel, a relay companion along the way.

Less spectacular but also extremely useful to the Indians was the spiky banana (datil) yucca, which was abundant higher up along the Grandview. Unlike the agaves, to which they're related, banana yuccas don't die after flowering. They send up a two-to-three-foot flower stalk that is densely covered with large, hanging, bell-like, creamy-white flowers with purple outer parts and a delicate fragrance. Their large, fleshy fruits appear by late summer. The Indians ate the fruits and used the yucca leaves for baskets, cloth, and sandals and their roots as soap and a laxative. Banana yuccas are the most common of the several species of yuccas found in the Grand Canyon. Each species is dependent on a particular moth for pollination. Even when not in flower, datil yucca is easily told apart from the agave. The edges of its leaves have curling fibers, whereas the margins of the agave's leaves have hooked thorns.

Agave rosette

Banana (datil) yucca

All these we noticed as we climbed the Grandview Trail steeply in the Supai Group along the west side of the ridge dividing Cottonwood Canyon on the west from the west arm of Hance Canyon on the east. In the late morning sunshine, the slopes of the Supai were subtly textured, the varied greens of the woodland plants contrasting warmly with the golden, rose-red and red-brown rocks and soil, all elegantly balanced. Across Cottonwood Canyon, the Redwall seemed to glow. The scrub of the Tonto Plateau far below appeared more green than gray. Down there, on the banks of Cottonwood Creek, there were vivid green clumps of tall cottonwood trees. Unseen, a canyon wren hung its rich cascading call on the silence. It seemed as perfectly proportioned to the quiet as the visual textures, shapes, and colors were to one another, everything restrained yet generous.

There were numerous washouts in the lower third of the Supai, but the route never required scrambling or cairns. Farther up, the Supai switchbacked steeply on the original cobbled trail construction, moving upward into the Hermit Shale.

We reached the contact of the Hermit Shale and the Coconino Sandstone at the saddle between Cottonwood Canyon and the west arm of Hance Canyon. We could look out at Coronado Butte. The trail headed west, switchbacking up the Coconino.

At the top of the Coconino, we came to the saddle between Grapevine Canyon and Hance—and stood briefly in a different world. At the head of Grapevine Canyon, mingling with large old pinyon pines, were tall conifers, the Douglas fir, which can grow to 80 feet here (and upwards of 200 feet in the Pacific Northwest). These pines—not truly firs, which their bark resembles, nor spruce, which their needles resemble—grow on shady, cool, north-facing slopes and form a microclimate for associate plants. Here the slope was indeed nearly north-facing. The Douglas fir are indicators that the climate of the Grand Canyon region thousands of years ago was cooler and moister than it is now, affected then by the glaciers farther north. The Douglas fir was sacred to the Hopi Indians, and they sent expeditions to the Grand Canyon to gather it.

Here at the Grapevine-Hance saddle there was a thicket of Gambel oak on each side of the trail. To the east we could see Sinking Ship, a slanting feature dividing the west and east arms of Hance Canyon. From here, the trail climbed up into the Toroweap Formation and switchbacked steeply upward, only reaching the Kaibab

Limestone a short distance below the rim. The Gambel oak stayed with us the rest of the way up, along with the pinyons, junipers, grasses, wildflowers, serviceberry, yuccas, agaves, and lots of pinyon pine cones. The cobbles and cribbing stayed with us, too. In many places logs were pinned into the side of the trail and crosswise to it, reinforcements installed by the park service in the 1970s.

When we reached the rim, we were exhilarated. We walked to the low stone wall at the edge to savor the splendid view from this aptly named point. In the distant west, Deva, Brahma, and Zoroaster temples; moving east, Wotans Throne and Angels Gate; then Krishna, Vishnu, and Rama; behind, the North Rim all the way east to Cape Final; and myriad other temples, points, buttes, walls, terraces, and valleys, each one of them seeming to be infinitely subdividable into more of the same-but-never-the-same. Closer to us: Grapevine and Cottonwood canyons, Horseshoe Mesa, Hance Canyon, Sinking Ship, Coronado Butte, Ayer Point.

We were sated with grandeur, and it was time to go. We loaded our gear into the car and drove 13 miles east to Desert View. There, we dropped our trash sack into a bin and telephoned the BRO to check in. We walked to the rim and looked out at a filament of the Tanner Trail and a regal sweep of river, green today, beyond it.

"Someday," I said.

Bob gave me a look. "The Tanner has no shade."

"But at the right time of year and if you cached water midway for the trek out," I said.

We stood there awhile longer, reluctant to leave. Finally, we turned our backs to the Canyon, returned to the car, and headed east for home.

Notes

1. From the GCNP Backcountry Management Plan, U.S. Department of the Interior/National Park Service, August 1983, pp. 36–37.

2. See appendix B, "Trails Data," for discussion of mileages on the Tonto Trail.

3. Not the same "mescal" as the globe-shaped, spineless cactus, also called "peyote," whose buttonlike tubercles were drained and chewed as a drug by some Indian tribes.

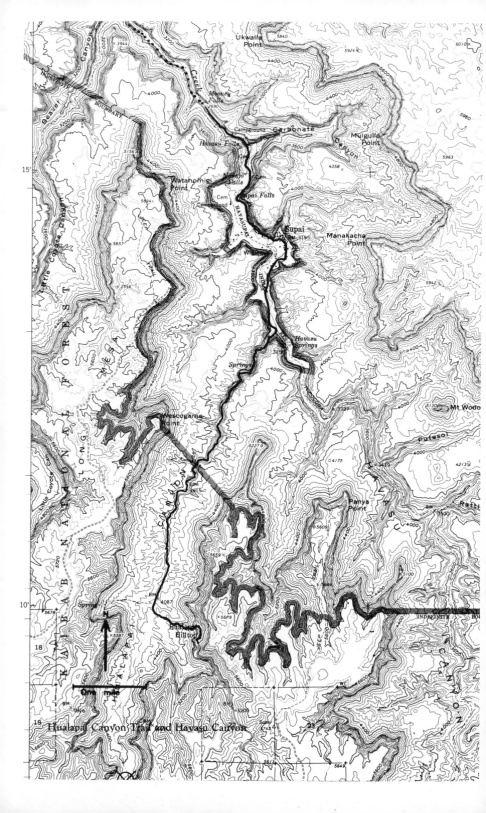

Hualapai Canyon Trail and Havasu Canyon

CHAPTER 3

Havasu
May 1982

The Hance-Grandview trip was pivotal for us. We'd had no physical problems, and, scary though the New Hance Trail had been,
we knew we were getting the hang of hiking in the Grand Canyon.
Of course we wanted to go back. I tried to figure out why.

The Canyon was becoming part of my interior landscape. When
I wasn't in it, it dwelled inside me. The glow that rose from its depths,
its vast and intricately defined space, and its engulfing silence at
first seemed to hold secrets not just of the earth's history but of the
mystery of my own consciousness and mortality. Yet the Canyon
didn't hold any clues to my condition; I just projected my own need
for meaning into it. I would have to continue to look inside myself
for answers. I came to accept that the Grand Canyon just *is*, and
that satisfied me. I understood that I wanted to be there just to be
there.

And so we planned another trip. The Tanner could wait (and,
as it turned out, wait and wait). We'd hike to the three big falls and
the turquoise waters in Havasu Canyon, the Havasupai Indian Reservation, and then do a loop on the Boucher, Tonto, and Hermit
trails with our friends Pat Hansen and Bill Whipple. We wrote to
the Havasupai Tourist Enterprise for camping reservations and to
the BRO for our permits at Boucher and Hermit. I continued to
do aerobic conditioning and always would. It didn't just make my
hiking more enjoyable. It enhanced my enjoyment of everyday life.

Bob and I decided to try internal-frame backpacks. Because they
fit the body closer than external-frame packs do, we hoped they'd

afford better balance on rocks and wouldn't bump or scrape against cliff walls. In the early spring, we rented internal-frame packs, loaded them up, and tried them out on the rough mountain trails outside Boulder, Colorado, 25 miles northwest of Denver. Parts of these trails approximate some of the conditions in the Canyon. The packs felt great, so we bought them. Wearing them in the Canyon turned out to be even better than we'd hoped.

We also did some boning-up on the Havasupai Indians, the "people of the blue-green water."

The Havasupais are thought to be descendants, along with the neighboring Hualapais, of the Pai (also called Cerbat), prehistoric Indians who came to the South Rim area from the valley of the lower Colorado River after 1150 A.D. The Pai farmed some, but primarily they hunted with bow and arrow and fiber nets and gathered food, fiber, and other necessities from plants. They were active traders as well. Eventually, a group split off, settled at Cataract Creek (later named Havasu Creek), and became the Havasupais. They farmed corn, melons, beans, and squash and constructed irrigation ditches not only in Havasu Canyon but also at Meriwitica Creek, Diamond Creek, Indian Gardens, and creek deltas in the Inner Gorge. They dried and stored part of their crops in sealed caves in the cliff walls, to use as food supplements in winter, when they lived on the plateaus, hunting and gathering. It was a balanced life that served them well, until the white man disrupted it in the late nineteenth century.

The Havasupais lived peaceably and traded with other tribes, including the Hopis to the east, from whom they obtained pottery and—after the Spanish colonization in the seventeenth and eighteenth centuries—horses and cattle, in exchange for their skillfully made buckskin garments, red ochre clay for body paints, and the agave, which was roasted for food in mescal pits.

The first written reference to the Havasupais was the report of Father Francisco Tomás Garcés, who came to Havasu Canyon in 1776 to convert the Indians to Christianity. The Havasupais welcomed Garcés but resisted conversion. Garcés is the first writer to refer to the river in the Grand Canyon as the "Rio Colorado."

Less than a century later, after the Civil War, increased settlement of the region by non-Indians led to conflicts, as the settlers' fences and livestock forced the game and the Indians off their traditional hunting lands. The Havasupais wanted only peace. In 1880, a 5-by-12-mile Havasupai Indian Reservation was established at Havasu Canyon, but the Army Corps of Engineers found the terrain too rough to survey accurately. The surveyor's report said that Chief Navajo was asking for a reduction of the reservation size, because he feared further encroachment and even eviction of his people from the canyon if the reservation had any significant size.

In 1882, the reservation boundaries were revised downward to 518.6 acres, which included only Supai Village and the croplands. The Indians were thus officially excluded from their traditional wintering grounds on the plateaus above, although they continued to graze their stock outside the reservation. In 1919, when Grand Canyon National Park was established and formally surrounded the reservation, the park superintendent immediately granted grazing permits so that the Indians could continue this use. Still, the stable old ways had been disrupted for good. There was malnutrition and disease, and many Havasupais found their way to Grand Canyon Village to work at construction and housekeeping jobs.

Meanwhile, prospectors came into Havasu Canyon and filed silver, lead, and vanadium claims. In 1880, one of them, Daniel W. Mooney,[1] attempted to descend to the bottom of a 200-foot waterfall, the tallest in Havasu Canyon. His rope was too short and he fell to his death on the rocks below. The Havasupais had formerly called the fall "Mother of the Waters" but took to calling it Mooney Falls, perhaps with pun intended. In the early 1900s, miners constructed tunnels, steps, and metal pegs down the cliff beside Mooney Falls, but they abandoned their claim there after a flood in 1910 wiped out their buildings and much of their equipment. Today, visitors use the miners' cliff constructions to get down to the enormous pool at the base of Mooney Falls.

On January 3, 1975, President Gerald R. Ford signed the Grand Canyon National Park Enlargement Act, which almost doubled the size of Grand Canyon National Park. Following the signing, the park covered 1892 square miles, the Havasupai Indian Reservation was increased to 185,000 acres, and 95,300 acres of "Traditional Use Lands" within the park were designated for the tribe. A 1982 "Memorandum of Understanding" signed by the Havasupais and the park service further defined the tribe's use and park management of these lands and clearly established rights-of-way for hikers.

Since 1939, the Havasupais have governed themselves by a tribal council. The War on Poverty made surplus food available to them, and the Bureau of Indian Affairs has helicoptered in prefabricated houses. Supai Village has electricity, and some households now have telephones.

The tribe numbers 400, about 50 of whom live in Winslow, Flagstaff, Kingman, and other towns in the region, working at odd jobs. The village school goes through the eighth grade and has a few dozen pupils, who are taught by non-Indian, certified teachers and Indian aides. There's a medic in Supai Village, and a doctor and a veterinarian come in occasionally. There are no roads or automobiles in Supai, and the mail comes in by packhorse.

The Indians farm and raise cattle, and they hunt during designated seasons, but tourism has become a mainstay of their economy. Twenty thousand people a year come from all over the world to see the waterfalls below the village: 75-foot-high Navajo Falls, named after the former chief; 106-foot-high Havasu Falls about 0.5 miles downstream from Navajo Falls; and Mooney Falls, 1 mile down from Havasu Falls.[2] Easter is the busiest holiday at Havasu. At Easter 1984, 500 people stayed in the campground that stretches from Havasu Falls to Mooney. As at Grand Canyon National Park, campfires are prohibited and visitors are required to pack out all their trash. The tribe also manages a general store, cafe, hostel, and lodge.

The Havasupais are concerned about overuse of the area by visitors. They try to limit the campground population to 250, and they strongly urge advance reservations, as they turn back visitors when all facilities are full. On reaching Supai Village, each visitor must register at the Tourist Office and pay a trail fee, which in 1988 was twelve dollars in summer, eight dollars off-season. The campground fee was nine dollars per person per night in summer, seven dollars off-season.

Supai Village and the falls are reached by foot or on rented saddle horse down the Hualapai Canyon Trail. The village is 8 miles and 2000 vertical feet from the trailhead, the falls 1.5 to 3 miles farther down the creek. The trailhead is located on Hualapai Hilltop, 61 miles north of U.S. 66 on a paved road. It's about 200 miles from Grand Canyon Village, via Highway 64 south to Williams, then west on I-40 and U.S. 66 to the turn-off, which is 5 miles west of Grand Canyon Caverns (7 miles east of Peach Springs). In the past, some visitors took the trail from Topocoba Hilltop down Lee Canyon and into Havasu Canyon, but this route was longer, and the 35-mile dirt road from Grand Canyon Village to Topocoba Hilltop was extremely rough and impassable during rains.

Bob and I expected our two-day visit to Havasu to be different from any other hiking we'd done in the Grand Canyon, for although we were going there to see the falls, we would also be guests of people of another culture.

May 30

We loaded up with water, left our lodging near Grand Canyon Caverns, and drove through Hualapai and then Havasupai lands to Hualapai Hilltop. There was no traffic, just sunlight and golden rolling plateau studded with pinyon pines and juniper trees and carpeted with purple flowers. Along the road were orange-blooming globe mallow, flowers that look like their name sounds.

We arrived at Hualapai Hilltop, keen with anticipation. And what a surprise there: a huge graded parking lot filled with seventy-five or more cars, vans, pickups, and motorcycles. It looked like a supermarket lot on the day before Thanksgiving, totally incongruous with the austere surroundings here in the Toroweap Formation. Of course: this was Memorial Day Weekend. There was a festive, even bustling air. People were organizing and putting on gear. A Havasupai wrangler was loading a pack train with supplies for the village.

We put on our packs, turned our backs on the twentieth century, stepped onto the first switchback, and came face-to-face with a Havasupai burro. He stood alongside the trail, grinning at us. Was he a descendant of the burros brought here by prospectors in the last century?

In the first mile we descended 1100 vertical feet through the Toroweap, Coconino, and Hermit Shale formations to the floor of Hualapai Canyon, which was in the Supai Group. From here it was an easy, straightforward walk northeast down the dry floor of the canyon. The upper section of Hualapai Canyon had an open feel. Its colors and textures contrasted pleasantly: green foliage of washside shrubs; cream-colored gravel; blocky, coarse, red-brown walls and boulders; prickly gray-green desert scrub on the clifftops, and a cloudless blue sky above. When we moved lower, the walls narrowed, and we knew this was not a good place to be when it rained.

It was almost a boulevard. There were visitors on foot coming up and going down and Havasupais on horseback. There was litter, too—wrappers, pop cans, plastic rings for six-packs. And there were "trail pups," friendly, pitiable dogs of indeterminate pedigree, undernourished, scraggy, with sores and rheumy eyes. They worked hard for a meager subsistence. They attached themselves to hiking parties and accompanied them for miles, hoping for food scraps. The hot gravel cut and blistered their pads, just as the friction from walking on it made our feet burn in our boots. Where did they go at night, these pitiful animals? Did they belong to any families in Supai?

We came to the junction with Havasu Canyon and the famous stream, flanked by cottonwood trees and willows. Havasu Creek emerges from the floor of Havasu Canyon about a mile above its junction with Hualapai Canyon. It has a flow of nearly 30,000 gallons per minute and is thought to drain an area of about 3500 square miles, from the San Francisco Peaks north of Flagstaff to Bill Williams Mountain at Williams and Mount Floyd northeast of Seligman. The water comes from precipitation that seeps slowly in a vast network down through the porous limestones of the Coconino Plateau, the plateau out of which the South Rim of the Grand Canyon has been carved. Where the floor of Havasu Canyon cuts down into the water-bearing rock, in this case the Supai Group at the Havasu Springs Fault, the water emerges and begins a 10-mile gambol to the Colorado River, nurturing a paradise of trees, flowers, birds—and the Havasupai Indians—along the way. The stream takes in more water at Supai Village.

As it trickles through the limestones of the plateau, the underground water picks up calcium carbonate, magnesium carbonate, and other minerals. The minerals settle out onto the creek bottom and, so long as they remain underwater, turn the bottom white. The white bottom of the creek reflects the color of the sky up through the water, giving it a bright-blue to blue-green appearance. When storms send water over the cliffs and down the side drainages, the brown sediments carried into Havasu Creek turn the creek brown until they are flushed out to the Colorado River. This was how we found the stream on our 1980 river trip, and it was devoid of the magic it has when it's blue-green.

When the mineral sediments are exposed to the air, they oxidize and turn rusty brown, forming a limestone called travertine, which in other locales is used as a facing material in construction—buildings in sixteenth- and seventeenth-century Rome, for instance.

The waterfalls at Havasu Creek display the two contrasting manifestations of the calcium carbonate and other minerals in the creek. The pools at their bases are blue-green, with clusters of semicircular brown travertine ledges, or dams, at their downstream edges. The cliff walls behind and surrounding the falls are of red-brown travertine, bulging with massive hanging aprons that look like they're covered with taffy and melted candle wax. The mineral-laden spray from the falls is blown against the cliff walls. When the spray evaporates, it leaves an infinitesimally thin coating of travertine. Over many thousands of years, the coatings have built up into these ragged curtains of stone that may be hundreds of feet thick in Havasu Canyon. Supai Village sits on travertine, and the falls are travertine falls over the Redwall Limestone.

From the distance, Havasu Canyon is brilliant with the color contrasts of water, cliffs, vegetation, and sky. Seen close up, though, the waterside vegetation and the campground are filmy with mineral dust and grit. Besides cottonwoods and willows, there are hackberry trees, box elders, wild grape vines, maidenhair ferns, crimson monkey flowers, watercress, and cattails. Robert Wallace, author of *The Grand Canyon*, a Time-Life book, lists these summertime birds at Havasu Creek: tanagers, swallows, swifts, warblers, hummingbirds, buntings, and goldfinches; at the pools, grebes, cormorants, kingfishers, teals, and great blue herons.

Instead of taking us alongside the creek, the trail followed an irrigation ditch that was probably centuries old. Soon we could see, on the canyon walls to the west, the Wigleeva, two rock pillars that represent guardians of the Indians and their crops. The Havasupais have traditionally believed that if those rocks ever fall, it will mean the end of the tribe.

A mile below the junction of Hualapai and Havasu canyons we came to Supai Village. It sat in a widening of the narrow valley,

Supai Village

hemmed in by the sandstone and shale cliffs of the Supai Group. Except for the absence of motorized vehicles, it might have been any sleepy rustic hamlet. It had small cultivated fields, dusty corrals with dusty animals, brown prefab houses, community buildings, and other rural constructions and detritus.

As required, we stopped at the tourist office. This was a busy place. Backpacks and visitors rested on the veranda. We went inside and presented the written confirmation of our camping reservation to the tourist manager, a man under a deluge of customers, papers, and cash. We paid the entry and campground fees, got our permit, and headed for the falls. Visitors and men of the tribe were hanging around the general store as we passed it. The trail zigzagged through the village and out the north end. Dust spurted out from under our boots as we and other visitors made our way toward the fabled falls, side by side now with Indians on foot—women and young girls with children, taking afternoon strolls. All the Indians we'd seen today were wearing Anglo dress.

We came to Navajo Falls, off to our left. It was very pretty, dropping into its blue-green pool in two sections divided by an expanse of travertine cliff. That's how it looked then. It could easily have changed since, as it has done many times, shifting back and forth across the cliff in response to the rearranging of its bed by the creek during floods. Our friend Jim Ohlman, who's a geologist and Grand Canyon trail guide, told us that most of Navajo Falls' water has been diverted eastward, drying up parts of the fall. "This natural diversion has deprived the fall of some of its former beauty," Jim said. "Actually, I find Supai Falls above Navajo more inviting. It's basically just a cascade, but it has several delightful wading pools."

We didn't know about Supai Falls then, so we continued down toward Havasu Falls, crossing to the west side of the creek. Havasu Falls has also changed since it was photographed and written about in 1900 by George Wharton James, a popular travel writer of the day. Back then, the fall was known as Bridal Veil Falls, and the photo of it in James's *In and Around the Grand Canyon* showed it fanning off the verge and across its cliff in a many-stranded veil. Not long afterward, a flood took out a huge chunk of its top, dropping the creekbed into the deep U-shaped notch it's in today and channeling the fall into the more unified appearance it has now. We were about to see if it lived up to its photographs.

Ten minutes later, a sight that made us gasp: off to our right, in a deep travertine bowl open on the east where Carbonate Canyon came into it, was Havasu Falls, dazzling, spectacular, better than its pictures. Its water leapt off the many-aproned cliff in a sparkling foam, nourishing mosses and ferns at its margins and tall cottonwoods around its pool. The pool was a gleaming blue-green, white along its upstream edges, with semicircular ledges of rough brown travertine below.

Havasu Falls was a study in illusions and incongruities: the astonishing blue that was color-where-there-was-no-color; the porcelain-white rock that metamorphosed into a pocked and pitted brown; the luxuriant greenery that grew in improbable profusion against the stark desert cliffscape. More: here on an Indian reservation, non-Indians disported themselves on the travertine dams and on a narrow beach with sparse grasses, looking for all the world like tourists at a tropical resort.

We followed a spur trail down to the pool and cooled our burning feet in it. We drank water, the water we'd brought with us this morn-

Havasu Falls

ing. The water in the creek must be purified, but there would be drinking water at fountains at the campground. Sitting with our feet in the pool, Bob and I talked about our feelings here. We were sorry that our society had disrupted the stable, traditional ways of the Havasupais. We knew that as a result of those disruptions, they needed our money, but we felt acutely that our presence here was not desired and only tolerated. We felt like trespassers. We admired the Indians' tolerance, which was greater than ours would have been in the same circumstances. There was no retrieving what the Havasupais or other Indian tribes had lost, and we felt a haunting sadness about it. Yet, perhaps they didn't feel that way. It was all very confusing. In the end, we knew that probably we could never understand.

We rested awhile longer on the "beach," took some pictures, and made a mental note to bring swimsuits if we ever returned to Havasu Canyon. Then we climbed out and headed for Mooney Falls, threading our way down the mile-long campground between the two falls, through dense bushes, across a couple of rivulets feeding into the creek, past drinking fountains and pit toilets and numberless campers. One look at the cliff constructions down to Mooney told us it would be better to descend without backpacks. We returned to the campground, found a site for the night, struck up a conversation with some campers adjoining it, and left our gear with them. Then we hurried back to Mooney with our camera.

Mooney Falls was also better than its photographs. Because of its extreme height, it didn't have the proportion and grace that Havasu Falls had, but it had power and drama. Its water sliced downward, boiling up a violent caldron of froth at its base and sending forth a loud roar. We tried to imagine the hapless Daniel Mooney being fooled by the height of the cliff, so that he used a rope fifty feet too short—another illusion at Havasu, and one typical in the Grand Canyon, where depths and distances fool the eye.

The pool at Mooney Falls was huge and the richest blue-green yet, but its downstream end lacked the charm of the one at Havasu Falls. Cottonwoods and bushes grew on a tan travertine island at the pool's lower end. Seen from above, the shallow stream channel on the west side of the island was not turquoise but tan streaked with green algae. A dozen people were lounging about on the island. We had fun on the crude jungle gym of pegs, chain rails, and metal steps that took us almost straight down the cliff to the pool. Bob decided to swim out to stand near the fall for a photograph. He took a position under a travertine umbrella that was decked with mosses. From where I stood, he was a pink speck, and Mooney Falls was too tall to be photographed full height. Mental note: next time bring a wide-angle lens, but even that still might not enable us to capture Mooney's brilliance and power.

On the island we met some campers from Los Angeles who were going on a day hike the next day about 2 miles down Havasu Creek to thirty-foot-high Beaver Falls, just outside the reservation, back inside Grand Canyon National Park. Only 3.3 miles up from the river, Beaver Falls was a popular side trip for river parties, although I hadn't made it there yet. On my 1978 trip, my friend Esther Johnston, her daughter, Karen, and I had been so entranced by some cascades and pools enroute that we'd stayed at them. In 1980 when the creek ran brown, Bob and I had lost interest. Mental note: next time plan to go to Beaver Falls.

It was time to return to camp. We clambered up the jungle gym and back to our site. Our neighbors had a visitor, a trail pup that couldn't have been more than four months old. He looked like a Norwegian elkhound. His stiff dark coat was caked with travertine dust and his eyes were sticky with mucous. He hung around our area for a while and then left, seeking his fortune elsewhere, another haunting element I would take with me from Havasu.

It wasn't a comfortable night. There were mosquitoes, and we used up almost all of our bug repellent. Travertine dust was everywhere and on everything. The campground was crowded, more like a barracks than a campground. Even with my ear stopples in—I'd brought them as a defense against exuberant frogs—I was kept awake by the loud snoring of a neighbor on the other side of the fallen log behind our heads. It was one of those wretched camping nights that you have sometimes, sleeping lightly and only in spurts, waking to hold the flashlight to your wristwatch (inside your sleeping bag, so as not to wake your companion, whose sound sleep you envy and resent), disappointed to find that it's only 10 P.M., 11:30, 1 A.M., 3:15. Trudging a quarter mile to the toilet in the middle of the night. Along about four o'clock you begin to panic. You've had too little sleep to feel very civil tomorrow, and morning is almost here. Then, from four till six, at long last, deep, restoring sleep. You'll make it through the day without snarling.

May 31

Up early and eager to depart the campground. On our way out we lingered awhile at Havasu Falls in the tender, slanting, early light. Bob took several more pictures. We regretted that we hadn't allotted an extra day or two to be at leisure in Havasu Canyon, but at the same time we wouldn't have wanted to spend another night like last night. Perhaps it would be more comfortable inside our tent, if it wasn't too hot. We passed through the village before the people's day was really underway and hiked on out. Again the incongruous parking lot; then the 200-mile U-turn back to Grand Canyon Village and a shower and a layover day waiting for our friends Pat and Bill to arrive for the Boucher loop. It would be their first experience in the Grand Canyon backcountry.

Notes

1. Mining records give Mooney's first name as Daniel, not James, as was erroneously reported by turn-of-the-century travel writer George Wharton James and numerous authors since. In his book, *In the House of Stone and Light* (Grand Canyon Natural History Association, 1978, p. 62), author J. Donald Hughes credits the correction to Helen Humphreys Seargeant, who wrote it up in her article, "Mooney Falls," in *Arizona Highways*, August 1959.

2. For a discussion of mileages, see appendix B, "Trails Data."

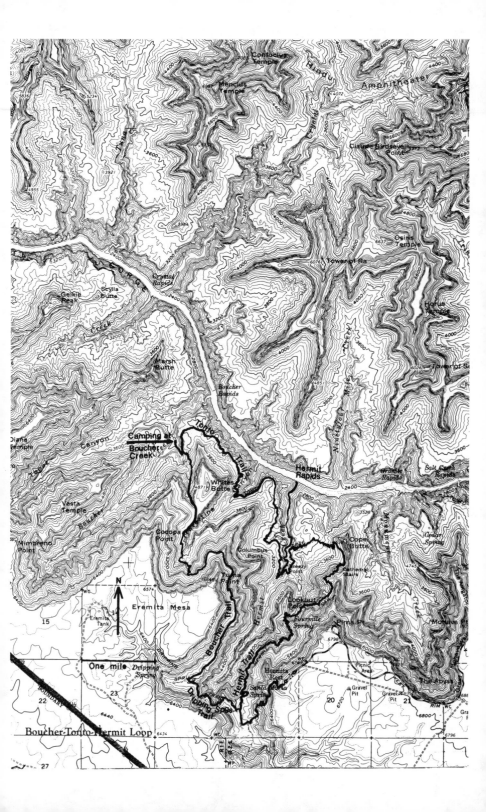

Boucher-Tonto-Hermit Loop

CHAPTER 4

Boucher-Tonto-Hermit Loop
June 1982

When you enjoy something immensely, after awhile you want to share the experience with friends. You can't just keep it all to yourself, and you want to be there with them so you can see their reaction. We were looking forward to that with Pat and Bill.

Before we'd left Denver, we'd filled our friends in on the minimum-impact practices urged by the park service to relieve pressures on the environment caused by the 30,000 hikers who spend 80,000 nights a year in the Grand Canyon backcountry and the additional 250,000 who do some day hiking there annually:

When hiking, stay on the trail. Don't cut switchbacks or roll rocks, activities that are destructive to the terrain and hazardous to hikers below. Any time you must leave the trail, walk on unvegetated soil or on rocks. Desert vegetation, once destroyed, can take decades to grow back.

Human waste and all personal and foodpan washing should be at least 200 feet from any water source, human waste at least 200 feet from any trail or campsite as well. Of course, this recommendation has to be tempered by good judgment: in some places, going 200 feet away may be dangerous for humans and harmful to the terrain. For bowel movements, dig a six-inch hole in as organic a soil as you can find, usually near the base of trees or bushes. Make your deposit, replace the soil, and take out your used toilet paper in a plastic bag; don't bury or burn it. For washing, use biodegradable soap and disperse the dirtied water on vegetated soil, again, 200 feet from water sources. If there's a toilet at camp, use it, and don't throw trash into the pit. Remember, you carry out what you pack in.

Care in selecting campsites is important in the Grand Canyon backcountry. Where camping is "at large," camp away from the trail, so that other travelers have uninterrupted wilderness along their way, unless there's a desirable and obviously established site along the trail. Try to camp on unvegetated soil or on bare rock. Do not alter the site: no trenches or rock structures; no cutting wood for lean-tos (and no campfires, either); leave vegetation in place.

If you're camping in a side canyon, your only site choice may be right in or near the creekbed. Remember the possibility of flash flooding, especially during the "monsoon season" (mid-July to mid-September), and try to stay high. Also, animals need to get down to the water, if there is any in the channel, so camp far enough away from the water to give them clear access to it.

When camping at the river, you should defecate into a six-inch-deep hole 200 feet from the water, but you can urinate in the sand at the river's edge. You can do your washing at the river, too, but don't brush your teeth in untreated river water. The river trips pack out all human feces, a practice which helps preserve the river and beaches for wildlife and for the more than 15,000 river travelers who stay 125,000 nights a year along it. It's safe to urinate at the river because a healthy person's urine is sterile (if it isn't, that person is in a hospital, not in the Grand Canyon), and the river volume is great enough to dilute and flush it away.

Where camping is in "designated sites" or in campgrounds, stay on the rock-lined paths in camp; don't cut across the fragile vegetated areas. And always, no matter where you camp, try to leave your site cleaner than it was when you found it.

When Pat and Bill arrived at the Canyon, we got our permit at the BRO, did last-minute grocery shopping, and organized our gear. We had to make a decision about shelter. May and June typically are the driest months in the inner Canyon, with less than half an inch of precipitation each. But I'd spent enough miserable, rainy nights under a tarp (including a downpour and flash flood at the mouth of Kanab Creek on the 1973 river trip *in early June*) to be reluctant to be without adequate shelter, just in case. Bob and I always carried our waterproof Gore-tex® tent, which weighs under five pounds. It can sleep three in a pinch. Bill had brought his four-person tent with rainfly, which weighed close to nine pounds. We decided to take only his tent. He'd carry it, Bob would take the poles, and we'd divide the rest of our gear to distribute the weight as fairly as possible. The BRO warned that the heaviest item in one's pack should be water. Since the Boucher Trail was long and water-less, we'd carry six quarts (twelve pounds) each, heavier than the tent.

At dinner, over huge salads—our last fresh greens for the next four days—we told our friends what we knew about the Hermit Trail and Louis D. Boucher.

Boucher (French pronunciation "Boo-shay") was "the Hermit" after whom the Santa Fe Railroad named the Hermit Trail, Hermits Rest, Hermit Basin, Hermit Camp, and Hermit Canyon or Gorge. He came to the Grand Canyon from Quebec, Canada, in 1891, seeking mineral riches. He may have worked awhile as a trail guide for John Hance, but eventually he settled at Dripping Springs, a dependable water source in an amphitheater on the western end of Hermit Basin at the head of Hermit Gorge. His home there con-sisted of two tents and a corral for his pack animals. He also had some sheep.

Boucher had a white beard and rode a white mule with a bell around its neck, which may have inspired the name he gave to the trail he built, the Silver Bell Trail (later named the Boucher Trail). It went from the rim to Dripping Springs and then along the west side of Hermit Gorge, around Yuma Point, across Travertine Canyon, and down Long Canyon (later renamed Boucher Canyon) to the creek. At his copper mine at Boucher Creek, he had cabins where visitors could stay and a large orchard and garden. He grew all kinds of fruits and vegetables, including peaches, oranges, melons, grapes, tomatoes, cucumbers, and chilis.

He wasn't strictly a hermit. He guided tourists and had men working for him. He had other mineral claims besides the copper mine, but none of them was profitable, and by 1912 he moved to Utah to work in a coal mine.

The Boucher Trail is not shown on the 1962 topo map, but it is shown on the BRO's Backcountry Trip Planner map. The rim trailhead to Dripping Springs is reached via a difficult dirt road.

Instead, the usual route to the Boucher Trail is from the Hermit Trail, and a wooden sign marks the junction of the Hermit with the trail to Dripping Springs and the Boucher Trail.

Our plan was to hike the next day down the Boucher Trail 9.3 miles and 3840 vertical feet to camp at Boucher Creek. On day two we'd hike 5.5-plus miles east on the Tonto Trail to Hermit Creek and take a side trip to Hermit Rapids, mile 95. Day three would be a day trip 3.5 miles east on the Tonto to Monument Creek, down Monument Canyon another 1.5 miles to Granite Rapids, a very powerful rapids at mile 93, and back to Hermit Creek for the night. The fourth day we'd hike out, starting early by quarter-moon light.

Things did not go precisely according to plan.

June 2

Another flawless day. Bright and early we rode the hikers' special to Hermits Rest. Pat was animated and nervous, I was excited, Bill was inscrutable, and Bob was serene. We put on our gear, walked down the service road and onto the trail through the trees. Abruptly, we began the steep and rocky switchbacks down the Kaibab, Toroweap, and Coconino formations.

I'd definitely come a long way since the first trip in 1979, and even since the New Hance Trail last year. The internal-frame backpack made a marked improvement in my balance, and I was positively overjoyed about that. Pat was new to backpacking, but she was a day hiker, dancer, and yoga instructor, and she was in excellent condition, with strong, muscular legs and good balance, so the trail wasn't as difficult for her as it had been for me three years before. Bill was experienced on all kinds of terrain and, at six feet, five inches, supple, lean, and at ease, like Bob.

Bill carried our flower book, Arthur M. Phillips's *Grand Canyon Wildflowers*, and "we" identified plants along the way: "What's this one, Bill? Bill, what's that? And that?" Easiest of all to identify was the ubiquitous cliffrose, a large upright shrub common from the rim to the Tonto Plateau, which we'd already seen in bloom on the rim. Its flowers were cream colored, with five rounded petals and a sweet, roselike fragrance. Our book told us the Indians shredded its bark to make clothing, sandals, and rope; the Hopis used it as an emetic and for washing wounds; and both they and the Navajos used its

wood for arrows. Cliffrose is an important winter browse for livestock and deer. It looks like the Apache plume, which is mostly
found lower in the Canyon washes, but plume is smaller and its
blossoms are pure white. Of course there was Utah serviceberry,
which we had identifed on the Grandview Trail last September. Now
it was in bloom with fragrant white flowers that had five long, narrow
petals.

Among the wildflowers were greenstem paperflower, a member
of the sunflower family that has a small disk surrounded by a few
broad, bright gold, three-lobed rays; hymenopappus, another sunflower, with rayless flowering heads, said to have been used by the
Hopis and Navajos as an emetic and to treat wounds; and numerous
other white, purple, and yellow daisylike flowers of the sunflower
family. Also there was orange globe mallow, another medicinal herb
used by the Hopis and occasionally eaten by bighorn sheep; red
Indian paintbrush, used medicinally and in ceremonies by the Hopis;
red penstemon; longleaf phlox in hues of lavender and pink; bare-
stem larkspur, vivid purple, containing chemicals harmful to cattle;
and purple lupine.

Our timing had been right, and we were delighted to see the
Canyon abundantly in bloom, and almost as delighted to be able
to identify what we saw. Funny business, this naming of things. Why
do we feel we know a thing just because we can call it by a name
someone else gave it? Is our appreciation of it really enhanced when
we add information to our experience of it? I had to admit that for
me it often is. Well, no harm in it, I thought, so long as we don't
let our passion for labeling things get in the way of our experiencing them directly.

We ate breakfast in Hermit Basin in golden morning sunshine.
Bob said he'd made a discovery, the same one I'd made early on
the trail: you don't have to suffer stiff legs for days after a Canyon
trek. All you need to do is go on another hike here right after the
first one, or maybe just spend enough days on the trail on the first
trip to work out all the toxins in the muscles. We'd suffered painful
legs after the Hermit and Hance trips. Today, our mild stiffness from
Havasu had vanished after the first dozen or so switchbacks.

Above us in the golden basin, flocks of blue birds darted back
and forth, calling sharply to one another—pinyon jays, named for
the tree because their favorite food is the seeds found in its cones.

I thought about how important the pinyon pines were to the Indians. They ate the sweet pine nuts and used the logs for shelter and the pitch to waterproof baskets and dress wounds. They used the juniper tree, too. Its bark made rope, roofing, fire tinder, even baby "diapers," and it shredded easily into a soft pulp for padding. The Indians also ate the juniper's puckery berries, which are actually modified cones.

As though she'd been reading my thoughts, Pat got up and wandered among the trees, looking closely at them as she munched a granola bar. Then she asked, "Which is pinyon and which is juniper?"

"Good for you for asking," Bob said. "We kept reading 'pinyon-juniper woodland' and felt foolish not to know which was which. Finally we looked them up. Utah juniper has the gray, stringy bark, and its trunk is sometimes twisted. The leaves are tiny and are pressed tightly to the stem like fish scales. And the juniper has berries. Pinyon bark has some red in it, and it has needles and cones. Do you see?"

"Yes, I see," she said, and sat down again. "What a relief to know," she teased. "Now I can rest my feet *and* my mind!"

After we finished breakfast, we prepared for hiking under the desert sun: we slathered on sunscreen and put on headwear. Then we started down the steep, rutted slope of the Hermit Shale and soon reached the fork and a wooden sign: left to Dripping Springs and the Boucher Trail, right to Hermit Creek. We went left and contoured across the head of Hermit Gorge for about 1 mile, until we reached the cairn-marked junction with the Boucher Trail at the Dripping Springs drainage, the western head of Hermit Gorge. We turned right and headed northeast in a long, rolling contour, still in the Hermit Shale, out along the west wall of Hermit Gorge.

Out, out along the wall, on wooded terrace above cliffs, taking our time. We fell into a congenial hiking formation. Bob took the lead, pausing occasionally to consider photographic possibilities. I was behind him, looking at flowers ("Bill . . .") and frequently urging water and trail mix on my comrades. Pat followed me, concentrating on staying upright, and long-legged Bill brought up the rear, stopping to identify flowers and check them off in the book, then loping easily to catch up with us.

Suddenly, an exciting find: a beavertail cactus in bloom, the upper ridges of its dusty purplish-green pads highlighted in coral and its pink blossom stretched platter-flat. The book said beaver-tail is most common in the hottest, driest areas, usually the Inner Gorge or the Tonto Plateau, but occasionally is found in higher elevations. This one was 2000 feet above its usual range. Bob took a picture of it.

We rounded Yuma Point, still on the sloping Hermit Shale. For a time we were more in the open. Agaves were blooming with spectacular twelve-foot-high stalks, their upper two-thirds covered with greenish-yellow, bell-shaped, waxy little flowers clustered on short stems radiating out from the spike. Large black bees were pollinating them. The ground was pink and rust, the cliff beside us buff and cream. Evenly spaced at shin height was grayish scrub—blackbrush—each plant a thick mass of tangled branches. Some sage and cliffrose, occasional pinyon pines. Everything was balanced, wide enough apart to share the minimal moisture in this thirsty landscape: desert detente.

Out on the point, we took a group picture with the Canyon opening wide behind us to the north, all in blues and pinks. We were delirious, greedy to record our moment here celebrating desert spring.

We looked to the east. Far across Hermit Gorge, the Hermit Trail headed across the Tonto Plateau, stayed right at the junction with the Tonto Trail coming in from Monument Creek, and switchbacked up the Muav Limestone on the west face of Cope Butte. We told Pat and Bill that would be our route out in three days. Pat's eyes grew wide. Bill took it all in, nodded, squinting, hands on hips. Below and to the left of the Tonto Plateau was the Inner Gorge. Its black walls, under the furrowed brow of the Tapeats Sandstone, were suffused with a pinkness. Seven hundred feet below the Tonto was a stretch of river, eerily but beautifully green, deprived of its sediments by the dam upstream. We could see the lower half of Granite Rapids and the bouldery island below it. There's an eddy at the top of the island that can keep a boat after it has come through the rapids. You just circle and circle, until it lets you pull free of it. A half mile above Granite Rapids was Salt Creek Rapids.

We took out our topo map and identified some of the named features across the Gorge: Confucius Temple, Mencius Temple, Hindu Amphitheater, Tower of Ra, Osiris Temple, Horus Temple,

Tower of Set, Shiva Temple, Isis Temple—names inspired by the grandness of their forms, or perhaps the metaphysical bents of those who named them.

We all agreed it was hard to translate the contour lines on the map into the scene we were looking at, because the distances in the Canyon are so deceptive. But once we got a fix on a really obvious feature from where we were standing, things began to fall into place.

Now it was late morning, and we realized we couldn't afford to continue in this leisurely fashion. Daylight wasn't a problem; there'd be plenty of that. Water was, or could become one. We could easily get low on water when we'd need it most—later, lower in the Canyon, in the hottest part of the day. We moved on at a more determined pace, contouring southwest on top of the Supai Group (still in the Hermit Shale) along the east side of Travertine Canyon, across a couple of short, exposed, heart-stopping ledges, until we reached the break for the descent of the Supai.

Now we were going to pay for the 4 miles of relatively level hiking since breakfast.

The descent of the Supai was almost straight down a boulder-clogged ravine on the east side of the head of Travertine Canyon. In a way, it was fun. Hard, but fun. Scree-y in sections, of course, but otherwise an unexposed clamber over, around, and between big rocks. The ravine was lush with trees, bushes, grasses, and flowers. We saw a couple of lizards and heard the canyon wren's hauntingly beautiful descending whistle.

Pat was daunted by the descent, understandably, since she was wearing an ill-fitted, borrowed pack that shifted loosely, but she managed it by herself, under the watchful eye of Bill. She had taken off her hat and tucked it behind the clip of her hip belt. Sunlight glinted off her silky blond hair. I'd made my point earlier about the importance of head coverings, and I didn't want to be overbearing. I hoped she'd have a greater tolerance for the sun beating down on her unprotected head than I did.

We had lunch in a clump of boulders at the bottom of the Supai, wedging ourselves in awkwardly to capture what little shade was available. We wondered how Louis Boucher brought mules down his trail, and we agreed we wouldn't want to go up what we'd just come down. It was so steep, you wouldn't be able to see the trail, such as it was, above you, and there were few cairns.

Pat reported she had a slight headache. Rx: fluid and food now; on the trail, *keep drinking water* – a good cup or two every fifteen or twenty minutes[1] – and nibble food with carbohydrates and minerals, like our trail snack of dried fruits and nuts. I mentioned the hat, and Pat put it back on. Before we started up again, I changed into long pants and a long-sleeved white cotton shirt. My legs and arms had begun to feel prickly in the sun, although the sunscreen had so far prevented a burn.

Now we began the descent of the Redwall. The trail was more of what we'd just come through, descending sharply part way down the main drainage of Travertine Canyon, then crossing the saddle at Whites Butte – a recent "toilet paper burn" here that would take years to mend – and dropping into the southeast drainage of Boucher Canyon. It continued steeply without a break down through the Muav and Bright Angel Shale (Tonto Plateau), and joined the Tonto Trail going down the Tapeats Sandstone to the creek and camp.

While we were still in the Redwall, Pat said she felt dazed. Bill looked worried. "Here, Patricia," he said, "drink."

We all drank and ate trail mix as we moved downward. It was a dry, baking hot now, a hot so desiccating, so stifling and still, you thought you might hear the air crack but heard instead the scratch of sharp twigs and the sickening slide of boots on scree.

We kept checking on Pat. Bill walked backwards to help her down difficult spots. Her headache grew worse and she became nauseated. She was sweating normally, though, and her color and pulse appeared normal. These were good signs. She was suffering from dehydration and mild heat exhaustion. The best remedy would have been for her to lie down in shade and to drink and take in salts of the trail mix. But there was no shade. Our best hope was to get her to camp, where, in addition to the cooling stream, there might be mesquite for shade.

Had she been sweating excessively or stopped sweating altogether and become flushed, with rapid pulse, we'd have had a life-threatening emergency on our hands – heatstroke, when the body's cooling system overworks and then shuts down entirely. I rehearsed in my mind the course of action: cool the victim in water, preferably a lake or stream, and massage her limbs to increase the flow of blood and encourage heat loss, until the victim stabilizes. The trip ends then and there, as heatstroke can recur. The victim must be taken to a doctor. We were more than a mile from Boucher Creek. If Pat had heatstroke, we'd wet her all over with our water, drop our packs and carry her as fast as possible to the stream, fanning and wetting her all the way. Tomorrow, we'd send for help.

Bill offered to take her pack, but she said she could carry it, wanted to carry it. She seemed rational, so we let her. I drenched her hat with water, thankful we'd brought plenty of it, and put the hat back on her head; wetted her scarf and had her wipe her face, neck and arms with it. I tried to get her to drink more, but she was too nauseated to manage more than some sips. She couldn't eat at all.

We reached Boucher Creek safely. Our sturdy Pat wept with relief for a minute or two, then lay on her back with her legs in the air. In that position, she removed her boots and socks, lifted her hips off the ground, and supported her back with her hands, in the yoga shoulder stand. She breathed deeply there while Bob and Bill stepped over to the creek and filled our water bottles. Pat recovered rapidly and was able to drink and eat and talk about what had happened to her.

"I just can't get over how easy it is to get dehydrated," she said. "You think you're drinking and eating enough, and still it isn't enough. First thing you know, you think you can fly. (Looks of alarm all around.) Really. When I was dehydrated, there were times on the trail when I wanted to lean out, spread my arms, and fly. I was disoriented enough to think I *could* fly. But my fifteen years of yoga practice saved me, because I instinctively knew to take deep breaths, and they kept me in reality. It was like there were two of me: one that was disoriented and wanted to fly; the other, deeper inside, that remembered to breathe to regain my center."

"I use my breathing on the trails, too," I said, "especially the exhalation. When I come to a scary place, I move out on my exhalation. I have to admit, though, I almost didn't deserve to make it across one of those exposed ledges on top of the Supai today. I exhaled just fine, but I stepped out on the wrong foot and nearly lost my balance; kept going, though, breathing. I was more scared after I got across it than I was before or during."

"I was never afraid of anything on the trail," Pat said, "not the exposed sections or even the scree. But I *was* scared about my knees. They swelled up from the pounding and the weight and shifting of the pack as I stepped off rocks. I was afraid my knees wouldn't hold out, but look, the shoulder stand brought the swelling down. I think they'll be okay now, so long as the worst of the downhill is over."

"It's over," Bob said. "The downhill will hammer your knees. It happened to me on the Hermit Trail, and although it was painful the whole hike out, my knee was well in a day or two."

Our crisis past, Bob and I walked downcanyon, our boots crunching in the moist gravel alongside the narrow, sweet stream, hoping to get to Boucher Rapids, mile 97, almost 2 miles away; but here, deep inside the Vishnu Schist, we were losing the light, so we turned back.

"Some other time," one of us said.

"Who said that? Aren't you the one who says at least once on every trip, 'Never again; this is positively the last trip; this is too hard'?"

"Some other time," someone repeated, smiling.

June 3

Leisurely start. We poked around Boucher's cabin and mine entrance at the creek before we left, trying to imagine him working his claim, tending his garden and orchard, guiding tourists, helping in a couple of river searches, and fishing in the Colorado River. Any or all of these in a day's work, so to speak; his routine for twenty years. Know-how, and no telephones, no boss, no income tax, no deadlines, little encroachment from the larger society on the rims and beyond. But oh, the commute between here and Dripping Springs! We stood looking in wonder at the mute evidence of his sojourn here, under great cliffs, at the seam of the Great Unconformity.

We struck out up the Tapeats Sandstone and onto the Tonto Plateau. The Tonto Trail would stay about 700 feet above the river all the way to Hermit Creek. We rounded Whites Butte on our way to Travertine Canyon and came to a head-on view of Hermit Rapids, 1.5 miles upriver, a symmetrical white chevron in the sparkling green

stream. The river was pressed to the north bank by the bulging fan
of the creek delta.

Up the dry wash at Travertine Canyon. It was bedded with slabs
of rusty brown travertine. There must have been a bewitching blue-
green stream here for a little while, say some tens of thousands – hundreds of thousands? – of years, and a shifting-around of
the earth or change in climate dried it up, causing the white travertine bottom to oxidize to these chocolate slabs. With its green shrubs,
it looked inviting still.

"This is one of those places you wish you could take the time
to explore as a side trip," Bob said.

"The Grand Canyon sure prompts a lot of visualizing of what
must have been," remarked Pat, who was strong and buoyant as
ever today, her knees sound, too.

We moved out the east side of Travertine Canyon, way out to
the verge of the Inner Gorge. The topo map showed the trail going
over a saddle back from the Gorge, but our trail stayed low and
wound around the outside. Typical of the Tonto routes to move
around, I thought.

We had one or two vertiginous views almost straight down at
the river. It muscled its way through the narrow channel, green,
deep, and mysterious. Close against the soaring cliffs of the Vishnu,
it flexed over and around unseen rocks and buttresses beneath the
surface and pumped up sandy eddies or boils, according to its own
secret laws. We watched them build, swirl, break up, and repeat the
cycle again and again. Grasses, flowers, and barrel cacti angled out
of creases and perched on miniature shelves in the black cliffs. There
were occasional small pockets of white sand high above the river,
left by subsiding waters after the tremendous spring runoffs in the
days before the dam.

Southeast now, up the west side of Hermit Gorge, around a
couple of side drainages. These 5.5 shadeless miles seemed longer
than they were, one of the distorting features of the trails in the
Grand Canyon. Chastened by our brush with disaster yesterday,
we ate and drank faithfully. You need to drink when you're not
thirsty, because if you do become thirsty while hiking, you've already
lost two to four pounds of water (one to two quarts) and are already
dehydrated.[2] Drinking and eating when you don't want to is a minor
inconvenience compared to the consequences of not doing so. The

BRO says people have been found dead of dehydration and heat-stroke with canteens full. After yesterday, that was more than just a mental picture.

We reached Hermit Creek by noon. We selected the campsite the couple from Florida had used in 1979, the highest one in camp, along a narrow shelf in the Tapeats. We called it "the Dormitory." Like all the sites, it was not far from the latrine, whose chemical odor pervaded the camp. We accepted that as an unavoidable neces-sity in a campground so heavily used. The Dormitory was the only site with any shade. The low wall of Tapeats on its east had an over-hang, and until midafternoon you could press yourself against the wall, cover your legs, and at least keep your head, arms, and torso out of the sun. During our stay, we'd invite people to come up to the Dormitory to perch like barn owls in its slit of shade.

And people there were, the first we'd met since we left the Hermit Trail yesterday morning. A few of them made a lasting impression. There were "the Swedes," four young men from Sweden, blond, well built and, as Bob characterized them, "just desperately healthy." They were camped below us, using a dome tent. They went about their business in a jolly sort of way that made us think of Snow White's team of dwarfs. Though we never spoke with them, we were glad-dened just by their presence in camp.

Also at camp was a hardy twenty-two-year-old drama student from Florida, a woman, hiking the Canyon alone. After the Hermit, she was going to hike the Tanner Trail, also alone. Hiking solo in the Canyon is risky and not recommended by the park service. Hiking the Tanner—9 waterless, shadeless miles that seasoned Canyon hikers say feels more like 12[3]—alone as summer tempera-tures were arriving could be extremely risky. She said she was going to start with eight or nine quarts of water and cache three of them on top of the Redwall for the trip out.

We spread our groundcloths and leaned our gear against the shaded wall at the Dormitory. We were eager to get down to the fall and pool below camp and later to go to Hermit Rapids. We quickly discovered, however, that we wouldn't be able to do that. Someone had to stay in camp at all times to shoo off our resident squirrel, who wasn't at all shy about approaching our gear. (He wasn't the only voracious squirrel in camp; we shooed them away from gear at other sites, but too late in one case, where a squirrel chewed into a pack before we could throw a rock at it.) There wasn't enough time, either, to do it all in two shifts. Moreover, the squirrels' presence meant we couldn't leave our things here tomorrow to go to Monument Creek and Granite Rapids as a foursome, as we'd planned.

Pat grinned mischievously, then sighed in mock regret. "I guess we'll just have to forego Monument and stick around here," she said, "and take turns at the pool and the rapids. Either that or carry our loaded packs with us to Monument."

We all grinned then, congratulating Pat on cogent reasoning that would save us 10 miles of shadeless hiking under backpack. Today we'd stay at camp and the pool; tomorrow we'd go to Hermit Rapids two-by-two and take turns at the pool.

Pat and Bill volunteered for first vigil. Bob and I went down to the pool. He found it just as delightful as I had, and we had it to ourselves, the other campers apparently having gone to the rapids

The pool and fall at Hermit Creek

or just down to smaller chutes and pools along the creek. We jumped in. The water was cold and the little fishes tickled us. It was paradise. Bill came down to find out what the whooping was about and took pictures of us frolicking there.

After an hour I returned to camp so our friends could have their turn. The only shade now was under a ponderous, low overhang above a slanting, flat boulder at the end of the Dormitory wall. I took water and a handful of stones, put my ensolite pad on the slanting boulder, propped my feet up on the shelf above its lower end, and lay on the pad with my face only inches below the overhang. Staying under that heavy slab was an act of faith, considering that Bob and I had seen a rockfall in the Canyon. But I knew that it wasn't *too* likely to collapse for a few more thousand years.

The squirrel came over to our gear. I chucked a rock at him: "tock." He retreated. It went like that for the next hour: Squirrel advances; "tock"; squirrel retreats. Advances; "tock"; retreats. Then: advances; I'm semidozing; squirrel chews into nylon sack containing trail mix; "tock"; retreats. Hole in bag, just like that.

Wedged into my crack of shade, I was learning something contradictory about a day at leisure at Hermit Creek. Its price was that you were chained, awake, to your gear by the need to protect it. Unfortunately, many unsuspecting or disbelieving campers would discover the price of leaving their gear unwatched before the metal pack bar was installed in 1983.

Bob came up to relieve me, and I rejoined our friends at the pool. Bill was standing waist-deep in the water, watching the little fishes nibble at his legs. Pat hauled herself onto the boulder across from the fall, stretched out her legs, leaned back on her elbows and lifted her face to the sun. "Mmmm," she murmured blissfully. "This is heaven."

I sat down on a boulder by the pool, wetted my scarf, and put it on my head. We were dreamily quiet for a while, and then Pat said, "I've been thinking about yesterday. Suppose I'd had heatstroke and couldn't continue the trip. What then?"

"We'd have had to arrange a helicopter evacuation," I said, "and we'd have been billed for the flight. For safety's sake, if the hiking party is big enough, two people should hike out together to get help, and at least one should stay with the victim."

The park service performs over 200 emergency searches and

rescues a year, usually evacuating victims by helicopter and some-times by mule or litter. Some of the "drag-outs" are in risky places, and the operations are costly. The park service spends an average of $100,000 a year on them. That's why the permit application ques-tions hikers about their experience, how much water they plan to take, and their emergency preparedness. It's also why they want hikers to stick to their itineraries.

"I've been wondering why you and Bob don't seem concerned about snakes or scorpions," Pat said.

"Because we aren't," I said, "but we're not casual about them either. Rattlesnakes are shy and really sort of rare along the trails that get much travel. Even Harvey Butchart wrote that he aver-ages seeing a snake about one day for every forty he hikes, and that's for the out-of-the-way places he goes. Scorpions also are around but seldom seen. They're nocturnal, and they hang out in loose stuff, like the debris at the base of bushes, under rocks, in crevices, and even in hiking boots and clothing. We just watch where we put our hands and feet, use a flashlight when walking in the dark, shake out our boots and clothes before putting them on, try not to camp too close to bushes, and we don't unroll our sleeping bags until we're ready to get into them. We also don't go barefoot in camp, even on beaches: the red harvester ants here can give you a nasty sting. Fortunately, they return to their hives at night."

"What would you do for a scorpion sting or a snake bite?" Pat asked.

"I'd try to stay calm and reassure the victim, especially if it was me!" I said. "And I'd quickly consult my pocket first aid manual for instructions. I don't think I'd take any chances trying to slash-and-suck a snake bite. That's a pretty controversial action that can make matters worse if you don't know what you're doing. And speak-ing of dangers from creatures: it's just good sense to avoid contact with rodents and bats. They can carry plague or rabies."

The sun was moving behind the west wall, and we returned to camp, cooked dinner and prepared for bed. We set our two groundcloths end-to-end and piled our open, empty packs and all our gear between us, hoping thus to keep night critters away. We lay on top of our sleeping bags and watched the bats come out to feed.

Night fell and the stars came out. Then the quarter moon rose, and we had a reprise of our first night at Hermit and last night at

Boucher Creek: the liquid-silver moonlight washed over the starlight and tinted the cliffs with platinum and gray. The frogs made a racket. The fall below camp shooshed and gurgled, and a balmy downcanyon breeze huffed and brushed softly over me. I abandoned myself to the sensations. But when I was ready for sleep, I put my stopples in my ears.

June 4

The Swedes were off early, we were told, for a day trip to Monument Creek and Granite Rapids. They'd left their gear inside their zipped-shut tent, and miraculously it remained undisturbed by rodents all day. Pat and Bill wanted to laze around camp before it got hot, so Bob and I took water, trail mix, first aid kit, and camera and headed for the rapids. A hundred yards below camp we came upon a prickly pear cactus with a crimson blossom. It was still in shade, so we planned to photograph it on our way back, hoping it would be highlighted then.

The water at the rapids was a little low. The river was running green, from days without rain anywhere in upstream drainages. A couple of raft trips came down, giving some of their participants the opportunity to stand on shore and photograph the others going through the rapids before it was their turn to ride. One of them was looking for Cindy, who was supposed to have hiked down to meet her there—tricky timing, to say the least. They didn't connect. Bob and I enjoyed a feeling of affectionate familiarity, being at Hermit Rapids for the third time since 1979. We felt as fortunate to be here now as we had both times before.

We rested awhile under some tamarisk trees at the mouth of Hermit Creek. They offered the only shade at the beach. The wavy-wanded tamarisk, also called salt cedar, is not native to the Grand Canyon or the United States. It's an exotic, low tree from the eastern Mediterranean. It was imported to California as a windbreak at the turn of the century and ever since has been spreading vigorously along western streams and rivers where, from March to August, it is covered with small pink flowers.

The tamarisk is rather a nuisance plant. It takes hold on beaches and begins to clog them, and it takes up and transpires enormous amounts of water. On the other hand, here in the Grand Canyon, where the river's beach-building sediments are trapped upstream in

Lake Powell, the tamarisk helps anchor the sand against the erosive force of tributary floods and thus helps to slow the decline of the Grand Canyon's beaches.

Bob photographed the crimson cactus flower on our way back to camp, and we took up our vigil at the Dormitory. Bill and Pat left for the rapids. We kept an eye out for squirrels at other sites and chatted with visiting barn owls. Bill and Pat relieved us when they returned, so we could go to the pool. The day grew hot as it moved lazily along in this side canyon that had formed over a period of six or more million years.

"Let's see," Bob said, scratching numbers in the packed moist dirt near the pool. "Six million times 365 days (forget about leap years): two billion two hundred million days have passed over this spot since it was a five-hundred-million-year-old rock layer buried deep under others, which changed to a gully, a ravine, a gorge."

"And how many of those days have you and I been on the planet?" I mused. "We're forty-nine and forty—average that to forty-five. Forty-five times 365" . . . scratch, scratch . . . "a mere sixteen-and-a-half thousand days. And so far only three of those days spent right here."

Bob erased the slate with his boot. "I like the one in Whitney's book,"[4] he said, "that compresses the two billion years since the beginning of the creation of the Vishnu Schist into a single day. The schist starts forming at 12:01 A.M. The Tapeats gets going around 6 P.M., and all the other formations are pretty much as we see them now by about 11:45 P.M. The river starts carving somewhere after 11:45 P.M., and human beings are on the planet at one minute to midnight. That could boggle the mind if you let it."

"It just doesn't throw me," I said. "The brevity of human existence on the planet doesn't bother me, because I don't think of us as being special or outside the process; I feel very connected to it. We're here, just as the trilobites and brachiopods and amphibians and ferns have been here in the seas and deserts that deposited the sediments and blew the sands that became these rocks. Maybe that's one thing the Canyon reinforces for me: the numbers are so immense—and anyway, time and numbers are just constructs of the human mind—that for me they exist outside of meaning. All that seems to matter is to really BE HERE while we're here and let the Canyon work its mysteries on us."

Late afternoon and everyone's back in camp, except the Swedes.

Ask the neighbors, shouldn't they be back by now? Finally, here they come, Heigh-ho, Heigh-ho, marching energetically back into camp. And everyone breaks into spontaneous applause.

June 5

Up at three-thirty and on the moonlit trail by four o'clock. As we climbed out the Tapeats and onto the Tonto Plateau, Pat said the moonlight gave her greater confidence on the trail: "I can't see all the rocks so I don't worry about them!" We moved comfortably across the Tonto, pausing now and then to look at the remote, surreal gray cliffscape across the Gorge. It was less daunting to me now than it had been in 1979.

We made good time, pushing up through the strata by moonlight, false dawn, dawn, and early morning, staying in shade until we were well above the hottest zones of the trail. Up in the Supai, the Swedes overtook us, bouncing along, Heigh-ho, in the bursting energy of youth and good health. For the first time we spoke.

"What time did you leave camp?"

Full of good will: "About six o'clock."

It was eight-thirty. They'd done in two and a half hours what we'd done in four and a half – and we were making good time! It computed about right: they were half our ages, too. (Time and numbers again.)

They skipped on ahead, Heigh-ho, leaving us laughing in their dust.

At eleven o'clock we were out, exultant. We dumped our trash sacks into a bin at Hermits Rest and rode the shuttle back to Grand Canyon Village. Then we piled into our friends' car, checked in at the BRO, and headed for a restaurant.

Notes

1. "Eat, Drink and Be Merry – Especially If You Exercise," by Gabe Mirkin, M.D., *Backpacker* Magazine, July 1983, pp. 76–77.

2. Gabe Mirkin's article.

3. Even though the Park Service has wheeled the Tanner Trail out at about 8 miles, most sources still believe it's closer to 9.

4. *A Field Guide to the Grand Canyon* by Stephen Whitney (Quill, New York, 1982), p. 242.

CHAPTER 5

The Corridor
(Maintained Trails)
Christmas 1982

Bob and I were curious about two things: what the maintained trails—the Bright Angel and River trails, the South and North Kaibab trails, collectively known as the Cross-Canyon Corridor or as just the Corridor—were like, and what the Canyon was like in winter. We decided to find out about both at Christmas in 1982.

The Corridor system was developed over the first four decades of this century and was designated part of the National Trails System in 1981. Its sometimes turbulent early history was influenced greatly by one man, Ralph H. Cameron, who tried to dominate the tourist trade at Grand Canyon Village.

The Bright Angel Trail (BA) was originally a bighorn sheep path. The Havasupai Indians used it to go from the rim 3060 feet and 4.6 miles down to the springs of Garden Creek at Indian Gardens, where they grew corn, squash, and beans. They were still farming there when miners began to use the route in the late 1800s. In 1890–91, a year before he built his trail to Horseshoe Mesa, Pete Berry, in partnership with the Cameron brothers, Ralph and Niles, and others, widened the Indian track and established mining claims at Indian Gardens. They soon realized there was richer ore in the wallets of tourists, so they established more mining claims in strategic locations so they could control access to the Bright Angel Trail and charge a toll for its use.

The trail was extended to the river in 1902, and by 1903 Ralph Cameron had bought out his partners and was charging one dollar for every mule-riding tourist descending the BA. (One dollar in 1903 would also buy 10 pounds of beef or 500 pounds of salt or two full-course dinners at a restaurant.[1])

Meanwhile, in 1901, the Santa Fe Railroad inaugurated its branchline service from Williams to Grand Canyon Village at the BA trailhead. This service lasted until 1968. The Santa Fe planned to build a hotel to draw more tourists its way, but Ralph Cameron built a hotel and located more mining sites on the rim until he controlled 13,000 acres and threatened to monopolize the tourist business. The Santa Fe developed the Hermit Trail in 1910–12 to bypass Cameron's toll.

From 1903 to 1926, Cameron was sued in turn by the Santa Fe Railroad, the United States Forest Service, and the National Park Service. In 1920, the United States Supreme Court invalidated several of his claims because there was no mineral of value on them, but he refused to give up, obstructing development by others until 1925 when, threatened with contempt of court, he relented. In 1928, Coconino County transferred the BA to the National Park Service (Grand Canyon National Park had been established in 1919).

On the North Rim, things were less complicated. In 1903, southern Utah businessman E. D. Woolley and his son-in-law, David Rust, began to develop the North Kaibab Trail down Bright Angel Canyon along a prehistoric Indian route. They completed the trail in 1907, and David Rust guided tourists down it on mules, putting them up overnight at his construction camp, called Rust's Camp, near the mouth of Bright Angel Creek. In the same year he suspended a hand-operated cable car across the river, and he built the old South Kaibab Trail from the river up to the Tonto Plateau. There it met the Tonto Trail, which went west to join the BA at Indian Gardens. A rim-to-rim trail system for tourists now was in place.

In 1922, the Fred Harvey Company, a subsidiary of the Santa Fe Railroad, built Phantom Ranch on the site of Rust's Camp as an overnight stop for its mule-riding tourists. Phantom Ranch continues to operate today.

The upper section of the South Kaibab Trail owes its existence to Ralph Cameron, although he didn't build it. In 1924, while Cameron still controlled Indian Gardens, the National Park Service decided to bypass the BA by building the new South Kaibab Trail from Yaki Point to the Tonto Plateau, where it met Rust's original lower trail. The new trail was completed in 1925, ironically the same year that Cameron finally gave up his Indian Gardens claim.

By 1928, the Corridor system included the Bright Angel, the South Kaibab, and the North Kaibab trails. There also was a new, rigid suspension bridge across the river, built in 1928 to replace a swinging suspension bridge across the river that had been built in 1921 to replace Rust's aerial tram.

During the 1930s, finishing touches were added here and there by the Civilian Conservation Corps (CCC), including the blasting of the 1.7-mile River Trail out of the schist of the Inner Gorge, linking the South Kaibab with the BA in 1936 and completing the Cross-Canyon Corridor system as it exists today, minus the Silver Suspension Bridge constructed in the 1960s.

Hikers spend about 33,000 nights in the Corridor annually. In addition, tens of thousands of day hikers travel the Corridor each year. So do mule trains carrying 10,000 tourists, trail maintenance crews, and mail and supplies for Phantom Ranch.

Bob and I planned to hike on our first day down the South Kaibab Trail 6.3 miles and 4780 vertical feet to the river and about another 0.5 miles to Bright Angel Camp for the night.[2] On day two we'd take the North Kaibab Trail 7.3 miles and 1600 feet up from Bright Angel Camp to Cottonwood Camp, stopping at Ribbon Falls enroute. Day three we'd hike 2.5 miles and 1200 feet up to Roaring Springs and then return to BA Camp for the night, an ambitious 12-mile day. Day four we'd hike out the BA Trail, 9.3 miles and 4380 feet to the rim. We sent for reservations well in advance, as even in winter the Corridor accommodations are much in demand.

Winter weather is unpredictable at the Grand Canyon. (Weather, in general, is unpredictable at the Grand Canyon.) On the South Rim, temperatures may be moderate to below zero, and the upper parts of trails are usually snowpacked and icy. The North Rim is closed in winter because of deep snow.

The average daily high at Phantom Ranch in December is in the mid-50s; average low, mid-30s. Average precipitation there in December is eight tenths of an inch, and Phantom Ranch gets some snow almost every year. Hikers are best advised to prepare for un-expected weather—to dress in layers and have wind- and waterproof outerwear.

In the end, weather changed our plans—the weather in Denver, not at the Canyon. A blizzard delayed our departure by one day. We called the BRO to ask them to hold our reservations. They said they would, but we couldn't change our itinerary: Bright Angel Campground was booked up. We'd have to reach Cottonwood Camp our first day — 14.1 miles, the distance from our home in suburban Littleton to downtown Denver.

Bob looked at me but didn't ask. "Should we go?" was not a question to ask a Grand Canyon addict.

December 27

We drove to the South Kaibab trailhead: out the East Rim Drive 1.1 miles from its junction with the South Entrance Road to the turn-in to Yaki Point; then 0.3 miles on the Yaki Point spur road to the trailhead turn-off (ample parking there) on the left.

We put on our packs and stood bundled-up at the snowpacked trailhead at eight o'clock under bright blue, windless skies. The temperature was in the teens. We stepped onto the trail. It was icy and steep, but underneath the ice the trail was smooth. We picked our way carefully down it, and within a few hundred vertical feet the ice was gone. It was easy walking from then on. That is, it was an easy walking surface, but it proved to be hard on the knees. The South Kaibab Trail has the steepest overall grade of any of the rim-to-river trails on the South Rim side. In addition, it is waterless and offers little shade. For these reasons, *the park service strongly recommends against going up it in the summertime.*

Because the trail is heavily used by casual hikers and first-timers in the Grand Canyon, the park service has installed cautionary signs that warn hikers to carry enough water, pack out their own trash, stand quietly for mule trains, etc. Other signs note the contacts between geologic formations and interpret the natural history along the trail. The Corridor trails are the only trails in the Canyon that have such signage.

Our descent began on the east side of the head of Pipe Creek Canyon. The trail headed north, switchbacking sharply down through the Kaibab, Toroweap, and Coconino formations, passing a microclimate that supported Douglas fir and giving fine views out into the Canyon. When we moved out beyond Yaki Point, we could see hikers heading down our trail to Cedar Ridge and O'Neill Butte. Farther west, we could see the Plateau Point Trail heading straight out across the Tonto Plateau to its lookout on the lip of the Inner Gorge, 1.5 miles from Indian Gardens.

At 1.5 miles and 1100 vertical feet, our trail entered the Hermit Shale at Cedar Ridge, a popular destination for day hikers and ranger-guided walks. It was a pleasant, breezy, open area with a pit toilet. On its western edge (the east wall of Pipe Creek Canyon) was an exhibit of fossil ferns from the time of the Hermit Shale's deposition in a vast river-floodplain environment 280 million years ago. The ferns were in their original bedrock, but under glass.

Below Cedar Ridge, graffiti was scratched onto boulders. We shook our heads in disgust. This was why glass had to be installed over the fossil ferns. The trail went northwest and entered the Supai Group just before the Cedar Ridge-O'Neill Butte saddle. We met a mule train coming up. Their canvas "panyards" were empty, indicating they had supplied Phantom Ranch.

The trail traversed north down through the Supai Group along the east side of O'Neill Butte. Three ravens soared beside the butte above us and chased one another raucously out over Cremation Canyon on our right. We had continuous, expansive views out into the Canyon, made possible because the South Kaibab Trail stays high along ridge lines.

Along the ridge below O'Neill Butte we met another mule train, empty like the first. Then the trail dropped eastward down the Red-wall in long, steep switchbacks, passing briefly, an interpretive sign informed us, through the Temple Butte Limestone. This formation is exposed sporadically as a thin purplish layer in the eastern and central sections of the Grand Canyon and continuously in grayish cliffs hundreds of feet thick in the western end.

Into the Muav Limestone. We took a sit-down break to rest our thighs and knees. We munched a snack and drank water and brought our attention closer now to the wide scallop of Cremation Canyon, which we were facing. Ranger Gale Burak told us that early white settlers found an open shallow pit with charred wood, bones, and artifacts on Shoshone Point at the head of Cremation Canyon. They surmised that the Havasupai Indians had cremated their dead and possibly pushed the ashes over the rim there; thus the name given the canyon.[3]

The scrub-studded Tonto Plateau swept out below us, creased where intermittent tributaries pushed water and debris into Cremation Creek. The long ridge with Newton and Pattie buttes on it angled north out from Shoshone Point, forming the eastern wall of Cremation's main drainage. Out of view and up that main drainage, Harvey Buchart wrote in Grand Canyon Treks, there are some caves in the Redwall, one of which was found to contain split-twig animal figurines, the earliest sign of human activity in the Grand Canyon. Such figurines were first discovered in 1934 in Stanton's Cave, a Redwall Limestone cave 140 feet above the river at mile 31.7, and have been found in several limestone caves since. They are believed to have been made by hunter-gatherers of the Desert Culture, Indians who inhabited western North America from 7000 to 2000 B.C. Similar figurines have been found in California and Nevada caves.

The figurines found in the Grand Canyon have been radiocarbon-dated at between 5000 and 3000 years old. Archaeologists believe the little deer effigies, some of them pierced with twig "spears," were a form of ritual magic to aid the hunt. There's no evidence anyone lived in the caves.

On our feet again. We passed a small rock quarry with green wooden dirt boxes lying around it—materials used in trail maintenance. The boxes are loaded with rocks and carried by mules to sections of the trail that have become rutted from use and weather. The rocks are dropped onto the trail and shoveled into the ruts.

Soon we entered the Bright Angel Shale (Tonto Plateau) as we descended northwest around the nose of the ridge separating Pipe and Cremation canyons, and here we had our first view of Natural Arch, 500 feet above us in the Redwall. It stood at the far right end of the Redwall outcrop, buttressed by a fin on its right side. The arch framed blue sky and a tree. It was a spare, lovely thing, probably around 30 feet high, and it stayed in view as we continued down the slope, until we turned north and met the Tonto Trail (another pit toilet there) and, a little farther, The Tipoff, so named because it's at the verge of the Inner Gorge (an emergency telephone there).

Off the Tip now, descending into the Inner Gorge, here a geologic mishmash created by numerous faults, down through Shinumo Quartzite, Hakatai Shale, Bass Limestone—members of the Grand Canyon Supergroup. The descent was dreamlike, down graceful, sinuous switchbacks that were never exposed, on trail that was neatly cribbed, rock lined, and dusty floored.

We heard the whooshing of the river now and saw autumn-gold cottonwoods lining Bright Angel Creek across the river. We paused at Panorama Point, elevation 3600 feet. It was aptly named, giving a dramatic view of the river 1200 feet below, the River Trail, and one of the footbridges over Bright Angel Creek. Across from us, the cliffs of the Inner Gorge were spectacular in the dry light: wrinkled, twisted, rugged, sheer, the black Vishnu Schist here was latticed abundantly with pink minerals.

Eventually we entered the same trellised schist as across the Gorge, and we marveled at descending with ease a trail blasted out of the same ragged, impossible cliff we saw across the river. A sign called it the Brahma Schist, but the sign was out-of-date. For a time in the 1960s, geologists tried to differentiate the ancient schists according to their inferred origins. Brahma was one of the tentative labels, but it didn't hold up under further study and was discarded. Vishnu Schist is Vishnu Schist, for hikers' purposes, anyway.

We were drawing closer and closer to the black Kaibab Suspension Bridge, and soon we could also see the Silver Suspension Bridge a half mile downriver from it. Then, the junction with the River Trail, a tunnel, and the bridge. It felt very secure, with metal rails and fencewire high on either side (they would reassure riders sitting high on mules) and heavy wood planks underfoot.

The Kaibab Bridge was built in 1928. It's 440 feet long, hangs about 75 feet above low water, and contains sixty-seven tons of structural steel, all of it packed down on mules. The bridge is guyed and supported by eight main steel cables, each one 550 feet long, 1½ inches in diameter, and weighing over one ton. It is stabilized by two "wind cables," which are connected by guys to the floor of the bridge and anchored at widespread points in the canyon wall at either end of the bridge. The cables couldn't be brought down on mules, so each one in turn was unreeled and carried down the South Kaibab Trail on the shoulders of forty-two Havasupais, like a gigantic snake. Because summer daytime temperatures in the Inner Gorge can reach 120 degrees, summertime work was done at night by floodlight. The old swinging suspension bridge remained in use during construction.

We stepped off the bridge and onto the North Kaibab Trail in a desert-beachy environment. The trail headed toward Bright Angel Canyon, skirting along a wall of Vishnu Schist, with the broad delta of BA Creek stretching out to the left. Ahead, the orange and gold leaves of the cottonwoods at the creek shimmered in the crisp late-December sunshine.

We came shortly to the 800-year-old Anasazi ruin discovered

by Major John Wesley Powell during his exploration of the Colorado River in 1869. On August 15 and 16, his party camped at the mouth of Bright Angel Creek (which he first named Silver Creek and later renamed Bright Angel). Powell found the ruin nearby, but it wasn't excavated for another century. It could have supported up to sixteen people and had two periods of occupation between 1050 and 1150 A.D.

The Anasazi (the word is Navajo for "the Ancient Ones") lived in the Canyon mostly in summertime and supplemented their farming of corn, beans, and squash with hunting and gathering. They abandoned the Canyon almost completely—more than 1000 sites—by 1150–1200 A.D. It's not known for certain why they left, but it's thought to have been because of drought. The Hopis of today are their descendants and are the most traditional Indians in the region.

Before we started this trek, Bob and I had known that in the Corridor we'd see everywhere the busy imprint of man. We could fairly easily "connect" with the more recent occupants—the farming Havasupais of Garden Creek, the nineteenth-century miners, the twentieth-century entrepreneurs. But standing before the Anasazi ruin, we found it harder to connect with the families that farmed here and then abandoned the Canyon altogether 800 years ago. It took an even greater leap of imagination to bring to life those remote, itinerant visitors, the makers of the split-twig figurines, who left the Canyon area 1500 years before the Anasazi ever even appeared on its rims.

Not far from the ruin we stopped in a sunny spot for lunch. We assessed our journey so far. We'd come 6.5 miles and descended 4780 feet; we'd walked backward two billion years in the earth's history and 5000 in man's. Not bad for a day's walk, but we weren't even halfway to our destination, and, sitting and resting here, we realized we were already feeling the wear and tear.

No point in thinking how wonderful it would have been to stop now at Bright Angel Camp, as we'd originally planned. Cottonwood was our assigned destination, and Cottonwood it would be. We'd have to set a determined pace in order to reach it while there was still enough light to set up our tent and cook dinner, but we knew it was important to be thoroughly refreshed before we started. We rested an hour and left just after twelve-thirty.

The mouth of Bright Angel Canyon narrowed, funneling the trail and creek side-by-side. The trail passed through huge clumps of prickly pear cactus, globe-shaped brittlebush, and clusters of the sprawling, poisonous sacred datura. In a marshy area there were reeds and cattails seven feet tall. The marsh gave off rich smells.

We passed the two footbridges that cross the creek to BA Camp (we permitted ourselves a longing look over there) and, 0.2 miles farther, came to Phantom Ranch. More than a dozen stone-and-wood cabins nestled cozily under cottonwoods planted by David Rust.

Phantom Ranch was designed for Fred Harvey by architect Mary Jane Colter. She also designed the building at Hermits Rest, the Watchtower at Desert View, and the Bright Angel Lodge on the South Rim. She designed her structures to be compatible with the natural and cultural environments, using native materials. The CCC built a swimming pool at Phantom Ranch in the 1930s, but it was demolished and covered over in 1972 because, here at the bottom of the Grand Canyon, it was too difficult to maintain to Arizona Health Department standards.

Above Phantom Ranch we settled into the business of getting to camp before dark. We decided to forego Roaring Springs tomorrow—that would save us 5 miles—and promised ourselves a leisurely 7-mile dawdle in BA Canyon instead, visiting Ribbon Falls along the way.

The trail stayed in the floor of the canyon and progressed through the Vishnu Schist and members of the Grand Canyon Supergroup—Bass, Hakatai, Shinumo, and finally the red Dox Sandstone, in which Cottonwood Camp is situated. Some of the beds were upturned or dipping and were threaded with igneous (molten rock) intrusions. These were the results of disturbances in the earth's crust along the Bright Angel Fault, which parallels the creek, crosses the river, slices through the upper Garden Creek drainage, and extends beyond both rims as well. We'd see the rock displacement by the BA Fault in the upper section of the BA Trail two days from now.

In our determination to make camp, we tried not to be seduced by sights along the way, but we couldn't help being struck by the side-by-side existence of the two plant communities in the canyon. A lush riparian (streamside) community thrived in and along the creek: algae, grasses, cottonwoods, willows. A short distance from the stream was the arid desert habitat with its cacti, yuccas, agaves, mesquite trees, and datura.

Above Phantom Creek, in "The Box," a narrows section more than 1000 feet inside the Vishnu, I saw a date palm on the west side of the creek. I'd never seen one in the Canyon and hadn't known they existed here. After our trip, we found a Grand Canyon Natural History Association booklet on the North Kaibab Trail that mentioned the date palm and confirmed that it's not native, speculating that its seed may have been dropped by a bird or a hiker.

The trail was always smooth and well fortified. It made numerous crossings of the creek on sturdy metal bridges, a far cry from the planks-on-rocks constructions of the early days. Often there were metal plates on the trail floor, markers for shut-off valves for the transcanyon pipeline buried beneath the trail that brings water to Grand Canyon Village. The pipeline was the solution to the most acute problem limiting the development of the South Rim: there isn't any surface water there, other than rainwater caught in natural "tanks."

Starting in 1901, the railroad hauled all water to Grand Canyon Village from Del Rio Springs, 120 miles south, and Flagstaff, 80 miles southeast. In 1931, construction began on a 2.5-mile, six-inch pipeline to bring water from Garden Creek up to the rim. A pumphouse of native stone was constructed at Indian Gardens. In 1932, the pipeline was in use and water trains were stopped, but by the mid-1950s supplies from Garden Creek were inadequate, and once again railroad tank cars carried water to the Village.

Finally, it was decided to pipe water by gravity flow 12.4 miles from Roaring Springs on the North Rim wall down Bright Angel Canyon, across the river on a new suspension bridge, and up to the pumping station at Indian Gardens. From there it would be pumped to the South Rim in the existing line. Construction of the transcanyon pipeline began in 1965. As it neared completion, on December 4–5, 1966, fourteen inches of rain fell on top of snow on the North Rim in thirty-six hours, sending thousands of tons of water and rock crashing down Bright Angel Canyon. This 1000-year "superflood" tore out bridges, wrecked the pipeline, and damaged the North Kaibab Trail. The creek stayed as high as thirty feet above normal for three days and stranded tourists and mules at Phantom Ranch. The pipeline was begun anew, buried beneath the bed of the North Kaibab Trail and finished by 1970, and it has provided a mostly dependable supply ever since.[4]

The transcanyon pipeline was possible because the walls of the North Rim have large springs and dependable perennial streams, whereas those of the South Rim do not. This difference is caused by the tilt of the plateau – called the Kaibab Plateau north of the Canyon and the Coconino Plateau south of it – through which the Colorado River has carved the Grand Canyon.

The entire plateau slants southward at one to two degrees, with the Canyon running across this slope. Groundwater percolating down through the limestones of the Kaibab Plateau flows southward toward the Canyon and issues generously from the walls of the North Rim. Groundwater also flows southward on the Coconino Plateau – away from the Canyon, so that the South Rim walls have only small springs and creeks. Havasu Creek is a notable exception; it drains mountains to the south of the Canyon.

Across a distance of 10 to 18 miles, the modest slant of the plateau creates a significant difference in rim elevations. The North Rim is 1000 to 2000 feet higher than the South Rim. It receives more precipitation, which erodes longer, larger side canyons and buries the North Rim under deep snows in winter.

It was fascinating to see firsthand all the geology and history we'd read about. But it was also becoming cold, and I was really dragging. Bob decided to scoot on ahead to camp to set up the tent. I plodded on behind, disconsolately dropping one aching foot in front of the other. When I saw in the distance the grove of cottonwoods at the campground, I took heart.

Bob came to meet me and insisted on carrying my pack the last few hundred yards. It was three-thirty when I sagged into camp. Already the light was going and it was much colder. By the time dinner was ready, we were fully bundled-up, awkwardly managing our meal in gloved hands.

After dinner, we hurriedly cleaned up and brought into the tent with us anything that we didn't want to freeze. We snuggled down into our sleeping bags (we'd brought our good four-season bags for this trip) right at dark, five o'clock.

Weary, grateful to be done with the trek, we reflected on the day. It had been beautiful, varied, and interesting, but it had been just too long a hike under backpack for one day. We suspected our fatigue could be a shadow over us for the rest of the trip, but we resolved to think positive thoughts to fend it off. (Bob would prove to be better at this than I.) As always, Bob slept soundly, but my cold feet (cold even with all my layers of socks on) kept waking me up.

December 28

The temperature was in the twenties when we awoke at daybreak, so we stayed in the tent until eight-thirty. It was sunny and we took our time, thawing bodies and gear and leaving camp around ten o'clock.

We headed 1.5 miles down BA Canyon to Ribbon Falls. A sign marked the spur trail leading to it, which crossed to the west side of the creek over a bridge. The fall is tucked into a short side canyon that receives little direct sunlight; thus, the fall is difficult to photograph. We got lucky, though, arriving in full sunlight. Immediately we dropped our packs and got out the camera.

Ribbon Falls is a good 125 feet high, a two-tiered travertine fall in the Shinumo Quartzite. It emerges from a slot, drops over a lip, then strikes and splashes over a huge moss-covered travertine cone. The fall creates a microclimate that supports maidenhair ferns, monkeyflowers, columbines, and shrubs. We thought it must be glorious in summertime, as even now it had great charm. Naturally, it's off-limits to camping, and hikers should stay on the established paths, one of which leads up onto the ledge behind the veil of the upper tier. Bob and I clambered up there and looked out, two specks squinting into the sunlight under a cobalt sky.

We spent a long while at the fall, resting beside its pool and basking in the sun's meager warmth, eventually eating lunch. We luxuriated in having it all to ourselves and in our lack of haste today, as, no denying it, we were physically overdone from yesterday.

After lunch we eased on down Bright Angel Canyon. Had this been summer, we'd have gone exploring up Phantom Creek (1 mile above Phantom Ranch on the west side of BA Creek). But that hike involves wading in the stream and, in the chill air, the risk of hypothermia—"exposure," the rapid chilling of the inner core of the body and the number one killer of outdoor recreationists—was too great. In temperatures below fifty degrees it's crucially important to stay dry, and it was barely forty degrees in The Box now.

Ribbon Falls, off the North Kaibab Trail

Two-thirds of a mile below Phantom Creek was the junction with the Clear Creek Trail, which enters from the east. Built by the CCC in 1933, it goes 8.7 waterless miles across the Tonto Plateau to Clear Creek, a perennial tributary of the Colorado River. Up in the Redwall in the northeast arm of Clear Creek Canyon is Cheyava Falls, at 400 feet the highest waterfall in the Grand Canyon. Its name is Hopi for "intermittent," as it only flows during spring snowmelt or after rains.

At last Phantom Ranch came into view, and at the sight of a *building*, all my brave resolve about positive thinking crumbled. I desperately wanted sound sleep and warm feet tonight!

I turned to Bob with my best piteous expression and asked, "Couldn't we see if they have room for us tonight?"

Lucky again. They'd had cancellations and had space in their dormitories. I would have loved to eat their hearty stew in the mess hall (I'd do that in November of 1984), but we wanted to lighten our pack loads. So we cooked our freeze-dried dinner and ate our pita bread and tapioca pudding outside the women's cabin.

December 29

I slept a wonderful, warm sleep and awoke renewed and full of enthusiasm for the day's hike. We hit the trail at eight-thirty, along with a handful of other hikers. It was chilly—low thirties— and overcast—a snow sky.

We crossed Bright Angel Creek and wound our way out through the campground, past the latrines and ranger cabin, past the ranch's sewage treatment plant (whirring sounds in there), past an empty corral, and onto the Silver Suspension Bridge, also called the Bright Angel Bridge. The transcanyon pipeline ran beneath the see-through, metal-grate floor of the bridge. Mule trains are prohibited on the Silver Bridge. They use the Kaibab Suspension Bridge and reach the BA via the River Trail.

Off the bridge, we followed the River Trail portion of the BA 1.2 miles west to Pipe Creek. The trail was a sandy ledge in the wall of the Inner Gorge that eventually crossed a sand dune. Not a comfortable place to be in the middle of a summer day. Wise hikers start before dawn or after 4 P.M. to avoid the heat here and in Pipe Creek Canyon. Going down the BA in summer, it's best to start at dawn or else rest at Indian Gardens until 3:30 or 4 P.M.

A sign said we were in Zoroaster Granite, a reference to the pink granitic intrusions in the Vishnu Schist. There'd be more and more of the pink Zoroaster in Pipe Creek Canyon.

The river swooshed through a rapids at the mouth of Pipe Creek. Across the creek, where it exited its gorge, sat the River Resthouse, a tiny knot at the bottom of the 8-mile Bright Angel string. It has an emergency telephone, but there's no potable water or toilet. Hikers are reminded not to take water from Pipe or Garden creeks because they are contaminated by the mule corral and sewage leach field at Indian Gardens.

We turned left onto the BA and climbed alongside Pipe Creek, crossing and recrossing it. No longer did we hear the smooth shooing sound of the river; now it was slurps and gurgles as the yard-wide creek spilled toward the river in small chutes and pools.

Pipe Creek received its name after Ralph Cameron played a practical joke on his brother, Pete Berry, and James McClure in 1894. They were traveling on the Tonto Plateau between Horseshoe Mesa and Indian Gardens. Cameron was ahead and found an old Meerschaum pipe in the streambed. He picked it up, scratched a date a century earlier on it and put it where they'd be sure to find it. They did, and they fell for the joke, wondering who might have been there so long before them. The story spread, and the stream has been called Pipe Creek ever since.

Garden Creek emerged from a narrow chasm on the west, after having plummeted more than 500 feet down from the Tapeats Narrows above, and joined Pipe Creek, becoming its major supply Above the junction, Pipe Creek was dry for a stretch and then re-emerged, quieter now, seeking the river in trickles. There was green algae in it, and riparian grasses and willows grew alongside. Farther upstream, the creek became scummy puddles of algae.

In a while, we saw across the creek from us a thin waterfall down a groove on the west wall. The telephone wires to the River Resthouse ran to the right of the fall. The fall was at least seventy-five feet high. A cottonwood tree stood at its brink and streamers of vegetation hung along its sides. This was the fall from Columbine Spring. In summer, it falls in a filigreed "X" pattern and is lined with mosses, ferns, columbines, and monkeyflowers.

Almost immediately after Columbine Spring fall we crossed Pipe Creek and began the ascent of the west wall of the canyon on steep switchbacks known as the Devils Corkscrew. Rerouted and reconstructed by the CCC in the late 1930s, the Devils Corkscrew is the only major zigzag in the otherwise southwesterly (river-to-rim) direction of the BA. Pipe Creek fell away from us as we climbed, its canyon heading southeast toward Yaki Point and the head of the South Kaibab Trail.

Upward, upward. I fell into a rhythmic breathing pattern – two steps on exhalation, two on inhalation, through lightly pursed lips. Ex(step) . . . hale(step) . . . In(step) . . . hale(step) . . . Ex . . . hale . . . In . . . hale. . . . I kept a slow, even pace, and the breathing helped me to climb; good rehearsal for the relentlessly steep 4.6 miles to come above Indian Gardens, and a pattern that would serve me well in all my hiking from now on. As I climbed, I was more and more thankful for last night's good sleep.

We began to sweat. We stopped for water and trail snack and to peel off a layer or two of clothing. Behind us on the Corkscrew, other hikers were stopping to do the same. We kept our wool hats and gloves on. From now on, they'd come off and go on, off and on, as we let our heads and wrists fine-tune the balance between body temperature and air temperature.

The pink-and-gray Zoroaster-and-Vishnu cliff we were climbing hosted a desert community. Yet, even here we were treated to more of the Grand Canyon's variety: seeps that supported mosses, maidenhair ferns, seep willows, and a cottonwood tree or two. High up, we crossed the small stream from Columbine Spring that feeds its fall, and we could see, far below, the cottonwood tree at the verge of the fall. The telephone wires ran alongside the stream.

At the top of the Devils Corkscrew we met Garden Creek, which cascaded down the cliff and into its narrow chasm. We climbed alongside and later above it, past chutes and pools and more cottonwood trees, moving upwards into the Tapeats Narrows. Anasazi Indians lived and farmed here seasonally; their ruins were on the other side of the ridge on our left. After them came the Havasupai Indians, who farmed here until this century, when the whites forced them out.

In the Tapeats Narrows, the streamside and desert communities existed side-by-side as they had in BA Canyon. It was colder in the shady Narrows, and the trail was less steep, requiring less effort. We started to cool down. Hats on, gloves on. Iron sky overhead and occasional sightings of Canyon features beyond the walls. Once, the museum at Yavapai Point hove into view. Our minds were set on reaching Indian Gardens, having lunch, and trying to stay warm as we rested. In spite of the cold and overcast, it was a good day. We were enjoying the Bright Angel Trail.

We reached Indian Gardens by eleven-thirty. There were a couple of dozen people there, and more were arriving. We plunked our gear at a picnic table near the water fountains, put all our warm clothing back on, and had lunch.

What history this busy oasis on the Tonto Plateau had seen. It had nurtured the Indians, sustained the miners and the pipeline builders, and given refuge to millions of tourists in this century; but not everyone had had the lush canopy of Fremont cottonwoods to shade them from the sun. These were planted in the early 1900s at the direction of Ralph Cameron — one truly beneficial legacy of this tireless, ambitious man. The shoots were brought from Cottonwood Canyon, 24 miles to the east on the Tonto Trail. Fremont cottonwoods are dependent on plentiful water, and they regulate their temperature by transpiring it. A single large tree can release fifty or more gallons of water a day.

Indian Gardens has seen another human enterprise, one that also depends on water: the photo processing lab of Ellsworth L. and Emery C. Kolb, two brothers who came to the Grand Canyon in 1902 and in 1904 set themselves up in the business of taking pictures of mule-riding parties starting down the trail, a business that thrived for seventy years. The water at the rim, which was then being brought by railroad, wasn't pure enough for photo processing, so the Kolbs built their darkroom at Indian Gardens, where they could take their supply from the springs of Garden Creek. This went on until the first pipeline was completed in 1932.

The Kolbs gained nationwide recognition for their 1911–12 boat trip down the Colorado River from Green River, Wyoming, to Needles, California, and for their motion picture of the expedition, the first ever made of a river expedition in the Canyon. For sixty years the film and lectures on the Grand Canyon were a feature of their business in their studio at the BA trailhead.

Ellsworth Kolb died in 1960, Emery in 1976. Their studio stands empty now. The park service owns it.

Chilly, and time to get going again. We left Indian Gardens and climbed moderately up through the Bright Angel Shale (Tonto Plateau), passing through dry drainages and eventually crossing the pipeline.[5] It was quiet here, the quiet of the desert. It was also dusty, and a mule train with passengers on a day's excursion to Plateau

Point kicked up even more dust. I was glad to be traveling on foot, in order to stay warm, rather than sitting and shivering on the back of a mule.

The trail stayed on the east side of the Garden Creek drainage. At the level of the Muav Limestone, the trail entered the Bright Angel Fault zone, which it would follow all the way to the rim. Faults are extremely important for travel in the Grand Canyon. Sheer walls like the Redwall, the greatest barrier in the Canyon, are impossible to breach without erosional breaks, which are usually made possible by faulting. Explorers in the late 1800s believed there could be only a handful of breaks through the Redwall, but Harvey Butchart knows 165. He's hiked them all and has discovered a third of them himself.

We ascended the upper Muav and most of the Redwall, still on the east side of the drainage, on steep, well-groomed switchbacks known as Jacobs Ladder. Ex(step) . . . hale(step) . . . In(step) . . . hale(step). . . . Now we could look outward and see the displacement across the Bright Angel Fault: on the wall to our west, rock layers were nearly 200 feet higher than the same strata on the east. Two ravens played rough-and-tumble out there, mocking the Redwall, hilarious over our heavy progress.

Ex . . . hale . . . In . . . hale. . . . Up the well-cribbed, pink-floored trail. Breathing frost. Backs getting damp. Hats off. In . . . hale. . . .

We passed Three-mile Resthouse (water there in summer and a year-round emergency telephone) at the contact between the Redwall and the Supai Group. Another train of mule-riding tourists, smiling stiffly through faces tight from the cold, came down.

The trail climbed relentlessly in steep switchbacks, but in spite of its steepness, it felt like home: we were back in the pinyon-juniper community. A few brown leaves remained on some of the bushes — serviceberry, hoptree, shrub live oak. There were rocks with lichen and, predictably this high up in the Corridor, graffiti. It seemed the graffitists only bothered to come down into the Supai Group on either the South Kaibab or BA trails.

After numerous switchbacks in the Supai, the trail made a long swing all the way to the west side of the Garden Creek drainage, then switched back. This was Two-mile Corner. We'd read that there's a large white boulder with Indian pictographs (paintings on rock) nearby. It should be uphill to our right on this switchback. We scanned the slope above us, not sure what we were looking for.

Bright Angel Trail and the Plateau Point Trail, seen from below the South Rim

Then we saw it, back on the east side of the drainage, about twenty feet above the trail. It was a chunk of Coconino, tumbled down from above, buff-colored, with a dark-stained overhang. On its trail-facing side were symbols in red ocher, believed to have been painted by Havasupai Indians. They knew where to find the red ocher, clayey substances used as pigments; they used it in trade with other tribes. We hoped the contemporary graffitists would spare this boulder if they saw it; they haven't spared the pictographs higher up.

Always now we could look outward at a broad Grand Canyon panorama, subdued under somber skies. We could see our trail and the Plateau Point Trail. We could follow the line of the BA Fault down the Garden Creek drainage and up Bright Angel Canyon. Somewhere up there, receding into the gray distance, was Cottonwood Campground.

In . . . hale . . . Ex . . . hale. . . . Stopping to catch breath. Cooling down. Hats back on. Resume.

We reached Mile-and-a-half Resthouse in the Hermit Shale (water in summer, emergency phone) and continued heavily upward, pausing more frequently to ease aching muscles. The temperature was dropping and was now in the low twenties, but fortunately it wasn't snowing.

Now up the Coconino Sandstone in more inexorably steep switchbacks. Several hikers were creeping about in a thicket of Gambel oak, cameras ready. In the thicket were two mule deer, a buck and a doe. We watched the aware but unconcerned deer and their conspicuous, patient stalkers and then moved silently on.

Almost home. Ex . . . hale . . . In . . . hale. . . . Through the Second Tunnel and into the Toroweap Formation. Patches of ice and snow appeared on the trail. Soon, Kolb Seep. It was a curtain of ice, but in summer it would be a magical, moist, mossy, grassy, dripping paradise set into a hillside microclimate containing Douglas fir.[6]

At last, the Kaibab Limestone. More ice and snow underfoot, temperature in the teens. Then the First Tunnel. So close now, only a skip (or a crawl) to the rim. But we stopped below the tunnel in order to see the Havasupai pictographs facing outward from a ledge at the rim, visible from here. There they were, spread along the narrow rockface like a modest banner, symbols in red ocher like those at Two-mile Corner; drawings of mule deer, too. Some of them had been vandalized with spray paint.

We stared upward at the rock paintings, then turned and looked outward at the Canyon scene they faced. What were they saying, and to whom or what were they saying it?[7] And for that matter, what were the vandals and graffitists saying, and *why?*

What a busy but tiny presence man had in the Grand Canyon, we thought. He could farm it, mine it, hunt in it, move water from rim to rim, travel through it on mule, on foot, or afloat, but there'd always be places in the Grand Canyon inaccessible and unknown to him and mysteries impenetrable by him. The pictographs seemed to affirm that, and Bob and I were comforted and elated by the Canyon's enduring, ineffable, inscrutable mysteries, which would always surprise and awaken the spirit.

We passed through the First Tunnel and up the icy trail to the rim. We surfaced, gray-faced from cold and fatigue but enormously satisfied with our trek.

Of course, we'd be back.

Notes

1. These examples of what a dollar would buy in 1903 are from

This Fabulous Century, Vol. I, 1900–1910 (Time–Life Books, New York, Revised 1978), pp. 141, 142, 144.

2. Tenths-of-miles for the Corridor trails vary, depending on what source you use. Elevations vary, too, depending on how you choose to read the contour lines at the river and particularly at the BA Creek delta. Precise numbers aren't important for hikers' purposes. The Bright Angel Trail includes the 7.8 miles from the trailhead to the mouth of Pipe Creek, 1.2 miles of the River Trail from Pipe Creek to the Silver Suspension Bridge, and the portion on the north side of the river to BA Campground.

3. The cremation practice may have abated after Father Garcés visited the Havasupais in Havasu Canyon in 1776, although Bill G. Bass, son of W. W. Bass (see chapter 6) said the Havasupais were cremating their dead in Havasu Canyon at the turn of the century (Stephen Maurer's *Solitude & Sunshine: Images of a Grand Canyon Childhood*, Pruett Publishing Company, Boulder, Colorado, 1983, p. 37). The practice appears to have ended sometime after that, and there are burial grounds in Havasu Canyon.

4. The transcanyon pipeline is subject to stress, rockslides, and corrosion. Harvey Butchart once met a crew that had come down to repair a leak. They told him they have to dig down and weld a new leak several times a year. Repairs can take a week. Storage tanks on the South Rim can hold up to a two-week supply during peak season while the system is shut off for repair.

5. This section of pipeline from Indian Gardens to the South Rim will be supplemented by pipeline in a slanting 5100-foot hole drilled through the Canyon wall. The new pipe will be connected to the pumping station at Indian Gardens.

6. Kolb Seep is believed to be from, or enhanced by, a leaky water pipe in the Village. At one time, there may have been some contamination from Kolb Studio on the rim, but its plumbing has been shut off for ten years, and, according to Rick Ernenwein in the park's Resources Management office, there is "no contamination coming from any source we know of."

7. Retired GCNP Librarian Louise M. Hinchliffe said there's nothing definitive on the Havasupai pictographs and that the "interpretation" of pictographs (paintings on rock) and petroglyphs (carvings on rock) in general is controversial.

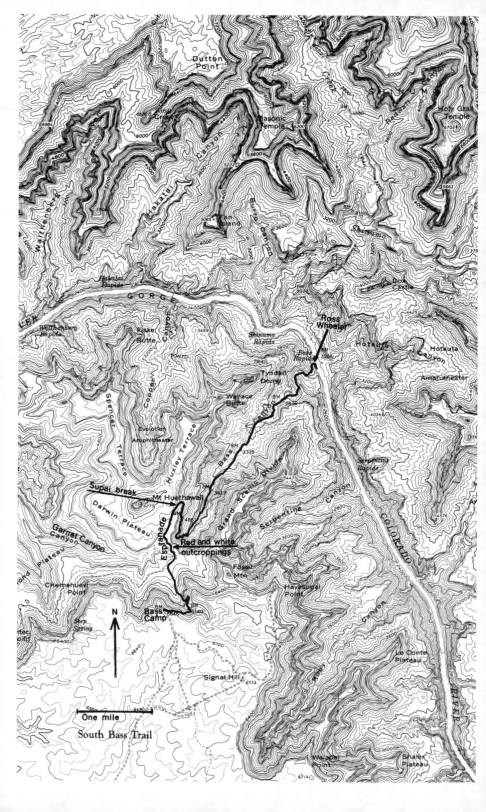

South Bass Trail

CHAPTER 6

South Bass Trail
June 1983/April 1985

June 10–12, 1983

Sometimes you just have a poor trip. It happened to us on this one on the South Bass Trail. And it was our own fault.

It started out well enough. The first part of the descent was easy. We were enchanted by the Esplanade, the plateau on top of the Supai Group that begins here and extends west in the Canyon, and we had no difficulty descending the Supai.

But somewhere in the Redwall the trip began to change. It was hot, brushy, and scratchy in the Redwall. The trail became harder to follow as we went lower. Bass Canyon was oppressive and eerie.

Then, trouble. We couldn't find the way to the river. We were low on water and we found ourselves on a terrace below the Tonto Plateau heading downriver away from Bass Canyon.

There was a cairn, but the faint route downward that it pointed to looked unlikely, a steep scramble down a rubble of boulders — but with backpacks on? This couldn't be the way to the beach. (The BRO had told us the beach was under water. The river was running high, as great flows from the tremendous 1983 snowmelt were being released from Glen Canyon Dam. We needed to reach the river for water, but we'd camp in Bass Canyon, per BRO recommendations.)

A knot was gathering in my stomach. We saw the river, saw Bass Rapids, mile 108. But we were above it, and the trail ahead stayed high.

We ignored the cairn and kept going downriver, but soon we

were past the rapids. The knot in my stomach began to tighten. Finally, we stopped.

"All right," Bob said. "This just isn't the way. We must have missed the right trail back in the creekbed." (We hadn't. A seventy-five-foot fall stops you at the river.) We decided that Bob would try the "unlikely" route at the cairn and I'd follow the trail back to the creekbed and search for water there.

We both found water. I found it in the bed of Bass Creek near where the trail climbed out of it: a few tiny, crystal-clear, tadpole-filled pools. And Bob made it to the river. It turned out that *was* the route.

We sorted it all out later, and we realized the fault had been ours: we hadn't done our homework. The map clearly showed the trail going west out of the bed, traveling across the terrace, and eventually reaching the river below Bass Rapids at the place where W. W. Bass had strung his cable across to Shinumo. It did not, however, show the cairn-marked spur to the beach. If we'd studied the map and our two guidebooks carefully enough before the trip, we'd at least have realized we needed to ask the BRO for directions.

We camped on ledges in the streambed, away from the pools. We hoped our presence wouldn't keep wildlife from coming to them. Bob was dehydrated but he wouldn't or couldn't recognize it. He was sullen and uncommunicative. It took some delicate persuading to get him to drink, but finally he did. When he recovered, he grudgingly admitted that maybe he had been a little dehydrated after all. Dehydration seems to affect the mental state of different people differently: Pat wanted to fly; Bob became sullen; and the two times I've been seriously dehydrated (both on river trips) I've found myself crying and behaving in a juvenile manner.

By now we were in no mood to appreciate our surroundings. Our original plan had been to spend two nights on the beach, 7 miles and 4400 feet below the rim. Now our alternatives were to spend a hot layover day here or to perch on boulders and watch the turgid, turbid river slosh by. But no beach. And no shade.

We decided to go back up to the Esplanade the next day and spend the night there. It was a good decision, and it salvaged our trip.

The Esplanade was magical. We camped under a large pinyon tree that sheltered a pineapple cactus with lavender blooms, and we spent the afternoon photographing flowers. That night, our tree

Prickly pear cactus on the Esplanade

shielded us from winds, and I named it the Guardian Pine. Beside it was a great old juniper tree whose branches intertwined with the Guardian's. I named it the Consort Juniper.

The next day we hiked to the rim and photographed wildflowers at Bass Camp until our hired ride (Fred Harvey Company) arrived to take us back to Grand Canyon Village.

We had planned to hike the Tanner Trail this trip. But having been thwarted by the South Bass, and realizing that it was already becoming too hot for the Tanner, we canceled and headed for home. Tanner would have to keep waiting.

White-tufted evening primrose at Bass Camp

In November 1984, our trail guide friend Jim Ohlman took a busman's holiday with me down the South Bass Trail onto the Esplanade. In his early thirties, Jim has already logged more than 8000 miles in over 800 days on foot in the Grand Canyon. A hiker's hiker, lean, tall, red-bearded Jim is capable, like his good friend and former math professor Harvey Butchart, of prodigious speed in the Canyon backcountry. He has a photographic recall of map contours, Canyon crannies, and vagaries of trail, and an immense knowledge of geology (he has a master's degree in it) and natural history. He has a gift for weaving it all together meaningfully and does so generously and with a wry sense of humor. And Jim has patience. He genially adapts his pace to that of slower hikers like me.

Jim showed me Indian ruins, fossils, and geologic features that Bob and I had missed or wouldn't have recognized. I revisited the Guardian Pine and its Consort and spent a bliss-filled hour resting near delicate bonsai gardens on the Esplanade while Jim climbed Mt. Huethawali (up and down a thousand feet in less than an hour!). It was a glorious day.

In spring of 1985, I backpacked the entire trail again with Jim's wife, Janece. It was her first trip back to Bass since 1982, and we both wanted to get the route clear in our minds. We got it right, right from the start, and it was altogether a joyous hike.

As always, to enrich our appreciation of the trail, we reacquainted ourselves with its human history.

William Wallace ("W. W.") Bass lived at the South Rim for forty years and was one of its most industrious and important settlers.[1] From the moment he first saw the Grand Canyon in 1883 — he was thirty-four and had recently come to Arizona for his health — he decided to live there and to bring others to see it.

Bass set up a camp on the rim west of Havasupai Point. He located asbestos and copper claims in the Canyon and improved an Indian trail down to Mystic Springs, from which he packed water up to his camp. Mystic Springs has since become unreliable and is not shown on the 1962 topo map.

Bass later extended the Mystic Springs Trail down Trail Canyon (since renamed Bass Canyon) and to the river, and eventually it came to be called the South Bass Trail. He built a boat at the river and used it to cross over to his tent camp, orchard, and garden a mile up Shinumo Creek, mile 109. Bass improved an Indian route from Shinumo up to the North Rim, which is now called the North Bass Trail.

He also constructed two cable crossings at the river, with cages big enough for his pack animals. The cables were removed in 1968 so as not to become hazards for river runners or helicopters, but Jim told me that remnants of the cable car at the Shinumo crossing still exist in a ravine on the south side, along with some exposed cable.

Bass taught himself photography, reportedly using a cave just below the rim as his darkroom. He was a friend to the Havasupais, employing them and helping to establish a school for them at Supai Village. For a time he provided mail service to the Indians, and he once went to Washington, D.C., to lobby on behalf of the tribe.

Above all, W. W. Bass was a tireless promoter of the Grand Canyon, for which he felt a great reverence. Around 1890 he built a road to Ashfork, 70 miles south of Bass Camp between Williams and Seligman, and brought tourists from there to the Canyon and into Havasu Canyon. He operated horsedrawn and later automobile-driven tours along the rim roads from the Village. He built a railroad siding 4 miles from the Village on the Santa Fe line to his own depot, and from there took tourists by buggy to Bass Camp.

The main house at Bass Camp stood less than 100 feet from the rim. The Camp could accommodate up to eighteen guests in the house and tent cabins. In addition, there were corrals and barns, a bunkhouse for the guides, and a warehouse. All of these have been removed by the park service.

In 1892, one of Bass's guests was Ada Diefendorf, a music teacher from New York. They were married in 1894 and had four children. Because water was scarce on the rim, Ada occasionally did her laundry at the river—a three-day trip.

W. W. and his family operated Bass Camp until 1923, when they retired to Wickenburg, northwest of Phoenix. He died in 1933 at age eighty-four and, according to his wishes, his ashes were dropped from an airplane over Holy Grail Temple, also called Bass Tomb, which is visible from the trailhead. Ada Bass died in 1951.

March 31, 1985

A beautiful morning, temperature in the forties. The Ohlmans' friend Dan Tobin drove us out to the trailhead at Bass Camp, 29 miles and ninety minutes northwest of Grand Canyon Village via Rowe Well Road and South Kaibab Forest Road #328, a rough dirt road nearly impassable during wet weather and best suited for high clearance, four-wheel-drive vehicles. Passenger cars can make it in the driest (which are also the dustiest) conditions, but risk bottoming out and losing their paint on the deeply rutted, narrow 3.5-mile stretch from the unmanned Pasture Wash Ranger Station to Bass Camp. The BRO provides detailed maps and directions.

Dan is a droll, burly, straight-faced twenty-year resident at the Canyon who knows some of W. W. Bass's descendants. He drawled stories about the area as we bumped and jostled along ("Sit still, Janece, you're rockin' the truck"). Dan's spent a lot of time in the Canyon backcountry and has seen his share of hikers' misadventures. In almost every case, he observed, panic has played the major role in their troubles.

"Your panic is your worst enemy," he said. "And lots of times it comes on because you haven't been drinkin' enough water."

It hit home. I told him about our scare on the South Bass in 1983.

"Like I said, your panic is your worst enemy. Sit still, Janece."

When we arrived at Bass Camp, Janece suspended one of our two-quart bottles and a small supply of food from a tree. If weather kept Dan from reaching us tomorrow afternoon, we'd have the cache to tide us over. I asked her why she'd hung the bottle.

"The rodents up here will gnaw even into a plastic water bottle," she said.

We spent some time at Bass Camp, letting the past soak in before descending into it. We imagined the structures and the comings and goings in this now silent place, where only the foundation of a cistern remains.

An Indian ruin stands at the rim, just a few paces to the right of the trailhead. Possibly it was built by the Cohonina—hunting-gathering-farming people who occupied settlements between central Arizona and the South Rim from 700 to 1150 A.D. but who did not inhabit the inner Canyon. It's thought they were the first to use the route to Mystic Springs and the river, and perhaps they built the granaries we'd be seeing in the Toroweap Formation. Or maybe the ruin and granaries were built by the Pai/Cerbat people, forebears of the Havasupais, who moved into the area from the deserts of the lower Colorado River after the Cohonina disappeared.

An iron pipe stands between the ruin and the rim. It goes down into a cavity immediately below, just off the trail. Bass dynamited the cavity for use as a cistern, connected by the pipe to rainwater collectors on the roofs of the buildings at Bass Camp.

Immediately to the right of the trailhead are two pinyon pines, here since well before 1900. There used to be a bench between them, where guests would gather to hear W. W. lecture. Or they'd sit there alone . . . sit between the Twin Trees, gazing out into the Grand Canyon, thinking their thoughts.

They gazed directly ahead at the domelike hulk of Mt. Huethawali (pronounced "Wath-*wah*-lee") – "White Mountain," the Havasupai name for its cream-colored Coconino sides and its Toroweap summit. Huethawali looms 1000 feet above the plateau it dominates. That plateau, 1500 feet below the rim, is known as the Esplanade, after which the uppermost member of the Supai Group, the Esplanade Sandstone, was later named.

The Esplanade is a nearly level platform on top of the sandstone, formed when the overlying Hermit Shale was eroded away. The Esplanade begins here, below Bass Camp, and extends westward to well past Havasu Canyon, mile 157. It exists on the north side of the river as well.

Off to the right of Mt. Huethawali is Bass Canyon, and its east wall is known as the Grand Scenic Divide, denoting the beginning

Mt. Huethawali, seen from Bass Camp

of the Esplanade here. The Grand Scenic Divide also signals another change in the Canyon topography: the petering-out of the Tonto Plateau at Garnet Canyon, mile 114, 6 miles to the west.

The gazers sitting on that bench between the Twin Trees would have looked straight ahead at Powell Plateau, an enormous platform on the north side, stretching to the left and right behind Mt. Huethawali. And the horizon on their left would be formed by Great Thumb Mesa, a South Rim feature that reaches out where the river, unseen from Bass Camp, makes a pronounced northeasterly bend.

One other conspicuous feature would have held the gazers' attention: the Coconino peak of Holy Grail Temple (Bass Tomb), elevation 6703 feet, on the north side of the river opposite Bass Canyon. It held Bass's attention, too, and, ultimately, his ashes.

Janece and I were ready. We said good-bye to Dan and started down the trail.

The trail began on the west side of the middle drainage of Garnet Canyon. The first descent headed east toward its head in an easy, unexposed, wooded traverse down the Kaibab Limestone, which in this part of the Grand Canyon has a rounded, sloped aspect, gentler than its blocky, turreted face to the east.

Some switchbacks, then we made the transition into the Toroweap Formation—still rounded, sloped, wooded—and eventually crossed the drainage and began switchbacking northwest along its east wall.

On this early spring morning, the woods were cool and smelled rich and moist, as the last patches of snow were melting. I remarked on how few junipers I saw along the trail, and Janece, a biology graduate, said, "You'll often see more pinyons than junipers at these higher elevations. Lower down, it'll often be the other way around."

"How can you tell them apart at a great distance, like here, where we can look down onto the Esplanade and out at the wooded slopes?" I asked.

"The junipers are more yellow-green, the pinyons deep green," she said. "Do you see it?"

"Yes," I said, "I see. Or I'm learning to see. When Jim and I came down here last November, he pointed out one fossil after another in the Toroweap. I can't find any today."

"It's hard for me, too," Janece said. "I think it's all in what you're trained to see."

The trail continued in the Toroweap Formation—doglike droppings of coyote here—skirting northwest along the top of the Coconino. Just before it entered the Coconino, we came to the first bay containing Indian granaries. They were fifteen to twenty feet above us, an easy scramble, tucked into ledges in the Toroweap. The closets were rocked-in, with rectangular entrances.

Jim had told me there are two prevailing interpretations of the granaries found in the Grand Canyon: one, that the Indians cached grains (chiefly corn), dried fruits, and berries in places they intended to pass through at a later date; two, that they stored surpluses to supplement their diets in winter if hunting on the rims was poor. In any case, Jim said, they built their granaries where they wouldn't easily be seen by others and sealed them carefully against animals.

Right after the granaries, we passed some barbed wire fencing beside the trail and just beyond it, above us in another bay, several more granaries.

We entered the Coconino, still heading northwest. The trail was a mess of rubbly switchbacks, more like the Hermit or the New Hance. Down we went, taking one or two wrong turns and retracing our steps. Then:

"Look!" I cried. "Here's the boulder with fossils in it that Jim showed me. I was hoping I'd be able to spot it by myself, and I did!"

It was a Toroweap rock about thigh high that had tumbled down into the Coconino and rested practically on the trail on the uphill side. It was loaded with brachiopods and pieces of horn coral from the time of the Toroweap's deposition in a sea 260 million years ago.

The trail continued northwest into the Hermit Shale, and now we looked back at the cream-colored Coconino Sandstone on the other side of the drainage. It was streaked gray with cliffwash and had large pocks in it, called "honeycombing," caused by the weathering action of wind and water. The contrast of the sandstone with the underlying rust-red Hermit Shale was sharp at their contact.

Mt. Huethawali loomed ahead as we approached the top of the Esplanade on the neck between Garnet and Bass canyons. The trail became obscure and was marked with cairns as we descended a succession of platforms, walking on remnants of the shale, among agaves, yuccas, pinyon pines, and sage, and coming down onto patches of the gray surface of the Esplanade Sandstone.

We came to a very large cairn with a rusty five-gallon can on it—from Bass's time? Soon after, we rounded the west side of a red outcropping and saw two low, circular mounds twenty feet across with small rocks and stones scattered on them: remains of mescal pits. Nearby, another.[2]

"This would certainly have been a good place for mescal pits," I said. "There's a lot of agave here. Jim told me he's seen mescal pits as large as 100 feet across." He had shown me how to spot them: an "unnatural"—that is, deliberate—mounding of stones in a wide circle. Not nature's way. Therefore, man's.

We cached two quarts of water and promised ourselves a long rest on the Esplanade tomorrow. Then we made our way toward the break for the Supai Group.

The trail on the Esplanade wasn't clear. Cairns marked it in a haphazard sort of way; sometimes a single rock at trailside was all. There were mule deer prints and more coyote scat. The main trail was braided with the search-tracks of other hikers—Jim calls them "crazed hiker routes."

But we knew you can't get lost on the Esplanade here. Once you're on it, you stay on the left (west) side of the outcroppings of red and then white rocks and then head diagonally (northeast) to the right of Huethawali through the trees and the blackbrush, to reach the Supai break. It's just over 0.5 miles in all.

If you bear too far to the right after rounding the white outcrop, you may end up at the edge of the Esplanade at the head of a precipitous ravine that spills down the Supai into the head of Bass Canyon. *This is not the trail.*[3] You can retrace your route or follow the lip of the platform northward around to where it eventually funnels into the trail at the Supai break down several short, erratic, cairned spokes. There's also a USGS benchmark on the left side of the break, 5376 feet, which is not shown on the map.[4]

Janece and I found the break easily and dropped down the Supai in northeasterly switchbacks. Then the trail doubled back south to the head of Bass Canyon. The trail in the Supai was a mildly exposed rubble of rocks and occasional slides. We tried to picture Ada Bass coming down it on horseback to do her laundry at the river! Below us, the Redwall formed the narrow, deep, brooding walls of Bass Canyon. They were grotesquely stained with cliffwash and broken in places from erosion along the Bass Fault.

At the head of Bass Canyon we entered the Redwall, and from

here on the trail would go down the canyon, crossing and recrossing the creekbed until it went west out of the bed for the final descent to the river.

The Redwall descent began on the west wall. It was an unexposed, brushy, cairn-marked clamber through large shrub oaks, curlleaf mahoganies, and serviceberries just coming redly into leaf.

This was where my trip with Bob had begun to turn, and it was easy now to recall why: the June heat had clamped down on us in the brush, and the dark-stained, dimpled, crumbled cliffs had been like blinders framing a narrow view outward. It had felt like a closet. Today was different. Janece and I had been drinking and eating and resting frequently. (I now always carried one water bottle in my hand, for easy access and reminder.) We were comfortable and our energy was good. The Redwall's bearded appearance, broken and blemished with some caves, was not unfriendly, and it framed a colorful, head-on view of Holy Grail Temple across the river.

We laughed to see a prickly pear cactus drooping off a ledge above us in the Supai like pearls on a string. Two canyon wrens called to one another. Clumps of hedgehog cacti snuggled on little ledges in the limestone, beginning to form buds. We could sense spring aborning, and it was good.

The trail left the west wall and entered the creekbed, still in the Redwall—sandy here, with wild geraniums greening the canyon floor. Down the bed we went, briefly. Very brushy and rocky. Then cairns led us up onto the east side of the wash, but we also saw cairns going down the middle of it. We climbed fifteen feet up from the bed on the east side and now could see a cairn on top of a boulder on the west side. But we stayed on the east, passing a redbud tree and—whiff!—a leafing hoptree, pungent with its skunklike, citrusy odor. Janece identified miner's lettuce and puccoon, a yellow flower that "belongs" higher up, blooming here a month early.

Still on the east side, we saw a pinyon pine, also below its normal range, and Janece said, "I like Redwall passages, because often, like here, they're in areas that get moisture and so have a great variety of plants from different life zones, like the puccoon and the pinyon."

Lower again, but still on the east side of the bed, swimming through tall riparian grasses that are members of the yucca clan. We dubbed them "shoelace yuccas," because they tripped us. One foot stepped on the ends of the five-foot-long blades and the trailing foot caught underneath them.

Eventually our trail climbed high above the bed on the east side, and we could see another path lower on the west side that appeared to go back into the streambed and end—a game trail?

So far, so good. We hadn't hit any dead ends. The South Bass was a route-seeker's delight or nightmare, depending on conditions and your point of view.

Done with the Redwall and into the Muav Limestone, staying high on the east side. Mostly blackbrush and some Mormon tea and agave here. Holy Grail's nubby peak perked up the otherwise flattish skyline, and Dox Castle began to come into view, in front of Holy Grail and to its right.

It was warmer here, and lizards came out to sun themselves and scuttle across the trail. We entered the Bright Angel Shale (Tonto Plateau) and crossed back to the west side of the creekbed. We came upon cairns marking the Tonto Trail-west at a point roughly across from the last bay of Redwall on the east wall. A couple of hundred yards farther there was a large cairn and a campsite at a small overhang on the west.

Cairns took us back across to the east side of the wash, still in the blackbrush. We entered the Tapeats Sandstone and quickly came upon a large cairn signaling the Tonto Trail-east. Our trail continued ahead, cut across a campsite, became briefly a bit faint and marked with cairns, then was clear again.

And now we approached the dark, ancient rock that gives lower Bass Canyon its strange brooding character. It was maroon, black, orange, and tan and had white lichens on it. It was blocky, wrinkled, and cracked.

"What *is* this rock?" I asked Janece.

"Jim says it's mostly Hakatai Shale that he thinks has been partially metamorphosed by later intrusions of the Cardenas Lavas," she said.

"Well it sure doesn't look anything like the Hakatai in Red Canyon," I said. "Here it's somber and eerie. In Red Canyon it's vivid and raw. I'd expected to find Bass Limestone down here."

"There's some of that, too," Janece said, "and even Jim says it's hard at a distance to tell this mixed-up Hakatai from the Bass Limestone. To make things even more confusing, there are some pockets of Vishnu Schist down here that have been brought up by faulting."

"Looking at this rock," I said, "I'm reminded of what Colin Fletcher wrote about the younger rocks higher up looking bright and smooth and young, and that you can just see them age as you descend into the Canyon. These rocks look crushed and heavy and ancient, almost like the Vishnu."

"The rocks progress—or regress—like this all over the planet," Janece said. "These old rocks are always warm, too," she added. "Even on a miserably cold, rainy day here in 1982, I picked one up and it was warm and it warmed my hand." We pressed our palms against a boulder and felt the warmth.

"Why is it like this?" I asked.

"I don't know. It just is. Jim speculates it could have something to do with the dark rocks absorbing more solar radiation and thus emitting more infrared, but I like to keep it simple and mysterious."

In front of us now was an impressive dipping fold in the dark Hakatai. The rock plunged into the ground from the east wall at about a fifty-degree angle, pinching off layers on the inside of the curve. We drew closer to it and soon stepped across its spine. It was a tapering, scaly, black-and-orange tail being dragged along the ground by some lumbering Halloween dragon. On either side of the dragon's tail were clumps of hedgehog cacti bearing dozens of the bright red, quarter-sized flowers that give the plant its alternate name: claretcup. It was another of the Canyon's surprises, a juxta-position of the friendly and young and the eerie and old.

We crunched along now on maroon gravel with tender new grasses and claretcups popping up everywhere and tons of lizards scurrying about. The warmth of the Hakatai seemed to animate them like so many windup toy Halloween dragons.

Unexpectedly, the trail took us into the creekbed from the east. This was a weird place, a flat, fissured moonscape of black-and-orange rock, small pools of water, wet sand, and dry falls, with cairns of white rock scattered across it leading vaguely to two trails on the west side.

Decision time: upper or lower trail? We took the lower and were lucky again. It took us around the dry falls and back into the bed. We guessed the other one was the lower route of the Tonto Trail-west, shown on the map, which eventually joins the upper Tonto-west.

And now things became even more strange. Below the falls, we recrossed to the east side and went out of the bed. Then the trail crossed back to the west. Then down into the bed. Then back along the west wall, but low, near the bed. Then into the bed again. Then recross to east side. Argh! This was definitely feeling bizarre.

"You could easily lose heart in here, and it's no wonder Bob and I did," I said. "All this back-and-forthing in this dark rock just isn't friendly."

"It helps a lot that we're not dehydrated," Janece said.

"Amen to that," I said. "I read that when Edith Bass was nine and her brother Bill five, they rode burros down this trail alone together to bring back some of their dad's horses from the river. Just shows it all depends on what you're used to. To us it's unsettling. To them it was home."

We saw another impressive fold on the east side, but instead of taking us to it, the trail brought us once more into the bed at some small pools. Cairns led to a trail going out the west side and away. That was the final leg to the river. At last, we were home, too. We found an established campsite out of the bed on the east side, dropped our packs there and hung our food from a mesquite tree. Then we took water and first aid kit and headed west to the river.

Light as lizards, we walked out along an eroded terrace and reached the cairn-marked spur to the river in less than ten minutes. Another ten minutes of scrambling steeply down the Vishnu Schist—it was a bouldery bluff here, not a ragged cliff—and we were on the beach. The scramble was certainly possible with backpacks on. It wouldn't be easy, but it wasn't very exposed.

On the way down, we passed the *Ross Wheeler*, a metal boat that was hauled high onto the rocks and left by a river expedition in 1915. It had nothing to do with W. W. Bass.

The boulders here seemed to stay in place by a common consent. They were smooth and occasionally rounded, enormous cobbles laced with pink Zoroaster Granite, nesting with brittlebushes, grasses and barrel cacti. Some of the cobbles near the water had sandy little depressions with pebbles and small stones lodged in them. In the days before the dam, during the river's spring flood, the pebbles would grind into their little cradles, polishing and rounding and deepening them. They had ground a fist-sized hole right through one rock.

Above the Vishnu bluff across the river was a broad terrace. Robert Brewster Stanton, running a surveying expedition down the river in 1889–90, thought the terrace would make a good place for a switchyard for a proposed railroad from Denver to San Diego through the Grand Canyon, one of many audacious schemes defeated by the Canyon.

Something struck me as odd: Bass Rapids began to our left, well downstream of the beach. I wondered about this and then realized that the modest rapids named for W. W. Bass probably was formed by outwash from Hotauta Canyon downstream across the river. In fact, there wasn't a rapids at the mouth of Bass Canyon.

The beach was lovely, a smooth, low shelf of pristine white sand. It had been reduced by at least half, Janece said, by the "flood" released from Glen Canyon Dam in 1983. Tattered shafts of tamarisk, shorn of their wavy plumage, stood among some rocks, stooped from the force of the flows. Bonelike shreds of bleached driftwood rested near the water's edge.

I walked up the beach to the mouth of Bass Canyon and looked up at the seventy-five-foot fall. Three small, stagnating pools stair-stepped down from its base. The beach extended upstream of the fall and then petered out into the gray rocks.

This was a serene, beautiful place. I realized with mild regret that Bob's and my travails in Bass Canyon could have been at least partially redeemed, even with the beach under water, if we had spent the end of our day doing what Janece and I now did:

We sat on boulders below the *Ross Wheeler* and watched the river go by. I made some notes and then put my pen and tablet away and let the peace flow into me. Toward sunset, full of contentment, we returned to camp.

April 1

Morning dawned sunny and crisp. Lying inside the tent, I listened to busy canyon wrens and a solitary owl. I reflected on yesterday's hike and the special qualities Janece had brought to it. She was a sturdily built, dependable woman, keenly intelligent, with a warm, gentle nature. And she had a quality of stillness. I had felt her stillness, her ability to relax and plug into her surroundings, as we had sat watching the river go by. She was below me on the rocks, and her entire form seemed to rest as quietly as the nesting cobbles around her. Janece was deeply attuned to the Canyon.

We struck camp early and set a slow, steady pace uphill. We rested, drank, and ate frequently, and our energy held. I used my Ex-hale-In-hale-Two-step on the steeper stretches.

In the Redwall we briefly found ourselves on a different, brushier route than the one we'd come down, tripping through dense "shoe-lace yuccas" and squeezing around boulders. Both of us recalled finding ourselves on this very same short alternate route, which quickly rejoins the main trail, coming up on our previous trips.

"How could one forget this?" Janece said, and we both laughed.

We met a couple coming down and reassured them about the crossings in lower Bass and the route to the river. They were our successors at Bass: the BRO permitted only one party at a time to camp in the South Bass "use area."

As we climbed the Redwall and the Supai, we paused more often. We may have been going slowly by others' standards—anyway, why rush?—but we still felt fresh and alert and were actually enjoying the upward haul.

We celebrated our arrival on the Esplanade with the long break we'd promised ourselves. We headed for the white outcropping, paying a visit to the Guardian Pine and its Consort Juniper and retrieving our water cache along the way.

We found the spot where I had rested, intoxicated by the forms, colors, and light, last November. We rested in silence. In *the* silence. It was so quiet, except for occasional pinyon jays or airplanes, that you could hear the blood coursing in your skull, and you knew that it was being driven by the same primal energy that was driving everything around you, including the rock.

Our backs leaned against the white boulders. At our feet was the gray Esplanade Sandstone, pitted by the same forces that had stripped away the overlying Hermit Shale and honeycombed the Coconino: wind and water. Their rasps were the tiny, colorful pebbles that rested for the time being in the gray pits they were making.

Countering their stripping effects were the cryptogams (crypto = hidden; gam = sex, reproduction)—microscopic plants whose fine, threadlike roots knit together loose particles of sand, forming a dark lumpy crust on the thin soil of the Esplanade platform. The cryptogams were the soil-binder that enabled all the other plant life here to get a roothold.

Cryptogamic soil is very fragile, easily destroyed by human feet, so it's important to try to stay off it. Once the dark, corrugated crust is broken, it can take decades to mend, and in the meantime the unprotected sandy soil is more vulnerable to wind and water erosion.

Here at the white outcropping, low mounds of cryptogamic soil supported small bonsai gardens. In one were agaves and grasses; another held sage, yuccas, and blackbrush with Mormon tea growing up through it. Here and there, rocks and pieces of deadwood accented the garden arrangements. Elsewhere there were rosettes of young agaves, cacti, cliffrose, curl-leaf mahoganies, shrub live oaks, pinyons, and junipers. In a month or two there'd be paintbrush and other wildflowers and cactus flowers.

It was an elegant, magical world—spacious, textured in soft greens and golds, pinks, rusts and cream, pervaded by a luminosity, and set off by blue sky and the mass of Mt. Huethawali to the north, Great Thumb Mesa to the west.

Too soon it was time to go. Dan would be at Bass Camp waiting for us at four-thirty. We left the dreamy pleasures of the Esplanade behind and set ourselves to the last steep pull. We reached the rim right at four-thirty and found a note at the trailhead. It was from Dan and it read:

"Had to leave at 2:30 P.M. Will be back at 8–9 A.M. tomorrow to pick you up. Left some food at Pasture Wash Ranger Station. Go ahead and walk there."

Janece was unconcerned. "Dan's a practical joker," she said.

We unstrung our water and food from the tree. I was grateful for the cache, considering our possible circumstances. At the tree we found another note:

"I'm really sorry about this and I want you to know the food at Pasture Wash is beans."

Janece laughed. That was the clincher. Dan knows she doesn't like to eat beans by themselves.

We saw him then, walking up the road with his stepdaughter, Jennifer, and his dog, Cowboy.

"Happy April Fools' Day," he drawled, letting a grin steal slowly across his face.

Notes

1. The W. W. Bass I read about in J. Donald Hughes's *In the House of Stone and Light* and Stephen G. Maurer's *Solitude & Sunshine* had little resemblance to the Bass that Colin Fletcher described in *The Man Who Walked Through Time*. Fletcher seemed to like Bass, but he romanticized him, favorably or not, as a "hairy malcontent" who only guided tourists "to make frayed ends meet." To the contrary, Maurer said that Bass made $20,000 from tourism in 1915 and at one time owned two houses, six surreys, and an automobile. Nor did he seem to be a "malcontent." Hughes and Maurer portray him as industrious, ambitious, and social, a trusted friend of the Havasupai Indians and a family man. Bass was a respected citizen of the South Rim, even if he wasn't liked by everyone. George Wharton James, writing in *In and Around the Grand Canyon* in 1900, spoke warmly of W. W. Bass.

2. The mescal pits are on the west side of the red outcropping. Faint trails come and go in this area, so it's not possible to say which side of the *trail* the pits are on. That depends on which trace you're following. We found them between the outcropping and our trail.

3. Jim showed me this spot—Harvey Butchart calls it a "climber's shortcut"—on the neck between Garnet and Bass canyons. The ravine eventually meets the trail just before the Redwall descent. It's occasionally been used as an uphill route to cut off a lot of traversing and switchbacking in the Supai, but Janece has gone up it ("almost on all-fours all the way") and said that even the climbers in her party needed to help one another in places.

4. I spoke to the USGS in Denver about the benchmark. They found it in their records of the 1902–03 survey and didn't know why it had been left off the map, where it would appear approximately under the "e" in "Huethawali."

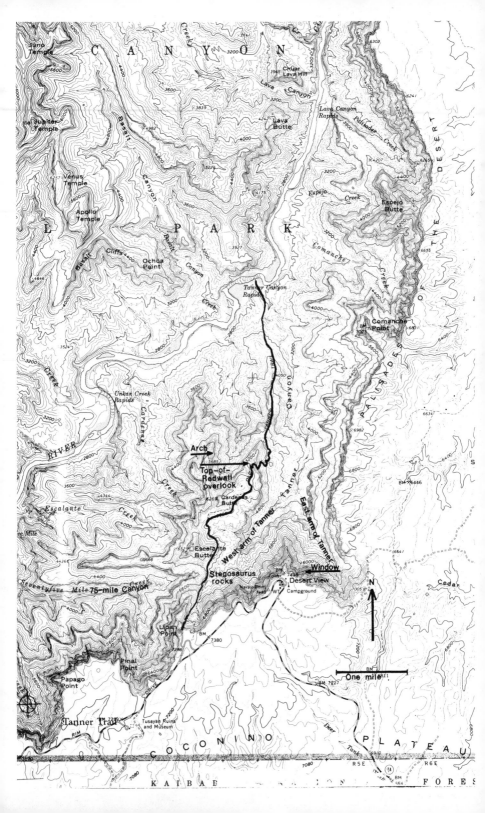

CHAPTER 7

Tanner Trail
April 1984

My friend Esther Johnston had been hankering to backpack in the
Grand Canyon ever since our 1978 river trip there. A veteran hiker
who also runs her own modeling agency in Greenwich, Connecticut,
tall, angular, long-striding Esther was always game for any outdoors
scheme I might have, and she knew she could always count on me
to have one. I did: the Tanner Trail (at last!), to be followed by the
Boucher-Hermit loop with a side trip west to Slate Canyon.

We'd go in April, before the summer heat bore down. We hoped
for a layover day at Tanner Beach (Tanner Rapids, mile 68.5), but
this was the Tanner's "season," and the BRO could only give us one
night there. It seemed a pity to rush it, but it is often a logistical
nightmare to match a hiking party's free time with travel and lodging availabilities and with whatever space the BRO has open. You
have to take what you can get. As it was, Bob had to be on a business trip during the Tanner, but he'd join us for the Boucher loop.

The Tanner area is associated with colorful lore and shocking
human disaster. The trail was originally an Anasazi route, used in
more recent centuries by the Hopi and the Havasupai Indians. In
the late 1800s, the white man came into the area to mine copper.
One of the prospectors was Seth Tanner, a trader living outside what
is now Cameron, Arizona, 30 miles east of the Grand Canyon. He
improved the route to gain access to his claims, and it became known
as the Tanner Trail. Tanner's main mine was upriver at Palisades
Creek, mile 65.5, and was known as the McCormick Mine, after
George McCormick, who ran it for him. Another prospector,

Franklin French, also used the trail, and for a while it was called the Tanner-French Trail.

Upriver, still another prospector, Ben Beamer, improved an Anasazi track from Palisades Creek up to the Little Colorado River, mile 62, and lived on an Anasazi site on the south bank of the Little Colorado, a few minutes' walk from its junction with the Colorado. His stuffy stone cabin is a popular day hike spot for river parties. The route from the Little Colorado all the way to Tanner Rapids today is called the Beamer Trail.

It's said the Tanner Trail was used by a gang of horsethieves operating in Utah and Arizona. They drove stolen horses into the Canyon, changed their brands, and drove them out onto the opposite rim using the Tanner Trail, the Beamer Trail, a river crossing, and the Nankoweap Trail on the north side.

There's also a legend that John Doyle Lee, who established his boat crossing of the Colorado at Lees Ferry in 1871, had a gold mine or had buried pots of gold in the Tanner area. Lee was executed by firing squad in 1877 for his alleged role in the massacre of 123 pioneers at Mountain Meadows in southwest Utah in 1857, and he took the secret of his gold, if there was any, to his grave. Many have searched in vain for it.

In 1928, park rangers discovered an abandoned distillery 3.5 miles up Lava Creek, across the river from Palisades Creek. Some people wondered if it might have supplied bootleg whiskey to Grand Canyon Village during Prohibition, but Harvey Butchart told me that when the still was found, its corngrinder was inoperative: it had been attached to the stump of a cottonwood tree, and good-sized saplings (perhaps ten years old) had grown up around the grinder, making it unusable. Harvey speculates that the still dated from the days of the miners and was abandoned when they left after the turn of the century.

It's intriguing to consider who did *not* use the Tanner Trail, for history might have been different if they had: the first white men to set eyes on the Grand Canyon. In 1540, a small band of explorers led by Captain García López de Cárdenas was sent into the region by Francisco Vásquez de Coronado. In his search for the fabled Seven Cities of Cíbola, Coronado had heard of a sizable river in the area and sent Cárdenas to look for it.

Hopi Indian guides led Cárdenas and his men to the South Rim of the Grand Canyon. From the expedition's description, the place they came to is thought to have been somewhere between Moran Point and Desert View. Cárdenas's men spent three days trying to get down to the river, until lack of water forced the expedition to give up altogether.

Had they wished to, the Hopis could have guided the Spaniards to the river, for they were in the vicinity of the Tanner route (its trailhead back then was east of Desert View), and the Hopis knew other routes as well. One of these was their ceremonial Salt Trail, down Salt Trail Canyon and the Little Colorado River to its confluence with the Colorado River and then a couple more miles downstream. Here they gathered the sacred salt that leached from the Tapeats Sandstone walls of both rivers. (The Tapeats is at river level here, the river having first cut down into it at mile 59.)

Most likely, the Indians wanted to keep the inner Canyon unvisited by outsiders, for the Grand Canyon is central to their religion. Their most sacred place is the Sipapu, a spring issuing from the center of a large travertine mound beside the Little Colorado River, 4.7 miles up from its junction with the Colorado. The Sipapu symbolizes the entrance to the underworld, from which human beings and animals emerged and to which the dead return.

The Hopis occasionally still hold sacred ceremonies in the area, and out of respect for the tribe the park service has closed the Hopi Salt Mines to all visitation a half mile both upriver and downriver from them.

Just across the river from the Salt Mines but centuries removed in their association with human history are Chuar and Temple buttes. On June 30, 1956, a Trans World Airlines Constellation and a United Airlines DC-7 collided over the Grand Canyon and fell onto these buttes, killing all 128 people on board. It was one of the worst commercial airline disasters up to that time. The bodies and eventually the shattered airplanes—as much of these as possible—were removed by helicopters. The Tanner area also has claimed the lives of several foot travelers, victims of their own panic and dehydration.

April 29

A sunny morning, temperature in the low fifties. We rode to the trailhead at Lipan Point, 20 miles east on the East Rim Drive from its junction with the South Entrance Road (or 2 miles west of Desert View, the east entrance to Grand Canyon National Park). The 1962 topo map does not show the Tanner trailhead in the correct place. It shows it on the Drive east of the spur road to Lipan Point. The trailhead is 0.4 miles *along* the spur road, on the east side; parking is 0.1 miles farther, at the viewpoint.

It was ferociously windy on the rim. We put on our packs and hurried to the more sheltered trailhead. The sign there said the trail was 8 miles long, but most other sources believe it's closer to 9, and from all we'd read and heard it would feel like 12. It loses 4600 feet of elevation.

We set out on the trail of horsethieves and Hopi Indians and immediately passed the cairn-marked left turn to the first switchback, following instead a faint old road. We quickly recognized our mistake, and after a twenty-second trip back to the cairn, we began the descent.

The trail began at the head of the west ravine of the west arm of Tanner Canyon, not, as the 1962 map shows it, in the ravine just to the east. It descended northeast in the usual rocky, steep switchbacks down through the Kaibab, Toroweap, and Coconino formations, passing through a large microclimate containing Douglas fir. Coyote droppings were abundant on the trail. In one place, recent scat rested on top of an older pile—territorial marking behavior, probably.

There was a good bit of hedgehog cactus up here, along with an abundance of buffaloberry—rounded, sometimes cascading evergreen shrubs with thick, oval, silver-green leaves that curl downward. A lot of boulders were covered with lichens, baseline creators of the soil.

Lichens are a combination of algae and fungi that grow extremely slowly on bare rocks. A single colony may be 1000 years old. The fungus part of them secretes an acid that breaks down the rock, widening cracks and producing crumbs for mosses to become established on. The mosses continue to break the rock down, leaving their own organic debris as well, until enough soil is present to support grasses, then large plants, and eventually trees. The process is aided by weathering, the breaking-down of rocks by heat, cold, running water, frost, and ice.

We saw wonderful examples of this progression along the trail. A boulder of Kaibab Limestone had a nine-inch-wide, elliptical hole six inches through it. Mosses and grasses grew on top of the boulder, which was encrusted with lichens. On another rock were lichens and mosses and a five-inch pine seedling. I liked the scaly, scalloped lichens because they came in so many colors—greens, browns, red-browns, oranges, mustards, black, smoke-grays, blue-grays, and white.

Our trail entered the Hermit Shale and traversed northeast down the west wall of the ravine. More coyote sign, more buffaloberry and lichens. Then it entered the Supai Group in a rough, rolling northeasterly traverse. The ravine widened. We looked out at Cardenas Butte and, to its east, the Palisades of the Desert, the colossal east wall of Tanner Canyon. Soon we could look back and see the Watchtower at Desert View on the headland between the two arms of Tanner Canyon. And now there was something else: the wind up the east arm of Tanner Canyon. We heard it blowing over there, battering itself against the Palisades, while the air in our ravine was still. We'd hear the wind from now on.

I wondered why it blew so constantly and found out a year later, when I rehiked the Tanner Trail with Jim Ohlman. He explained that canyon walls heat up during the day, and hot air rises along and up them. When the air rises high enough, it cools, and, cool air being heavier than warm air, the air descends. So there's a circulation of air. At night, the reverse occurs, with cool air descending along tributary walls to the river, thus accounting for the down-canyon breezes you feel, say, at Hermit Creek, in the evening.

"Air doesn't really strike against the canyon walls," Jim said, "but rather ascends or descends along them—although it's hard to prove this while getting blown off Seventy-five Mile Saddle along the Tanner Trail!" Esther and I were about to find this out for ourselves.

As we continued in the Supai Group out the west wall of the ravine, Escalante Butte moved into view from the left, its rhythmic pyramidal masses eventually blocking the view of Cardenas Butte. We came out on a very small point, called a "nick point," and had our first view west into the Canyon at Vishnu Temple, Wotans Throne, Angels Gate, Zoroaster Temple, and Shiva Temple. Below us on the low west ridge of Escalante was a small butte shown only as elevation 5666 feet on the map. Jim later told me it's known locally as Wedding Cake Butte, which indeed is what it looked like.

Here on this nick point we were also looking down onto Seventy-five Mile Saddle, the neck at the base of Escalante Butte between Seventy-five Mile and Tanner canyons. The Thybony guide says that one branch of the trail stays high and goes across the ridge-line of the saddle, and another goes down into our ravine. But in fact, there didn't appear to be a higher route, and it looked like a difficult way to go. The trail was clearly marked for a sharp right turn downward.

We turned right, switchbacked down to the floor of the ravine, and stayed there briefly. There were brushy shrubs and lots more coyote sign, and two canyon wrens cheeping at each other. Then the trail climbed back up the west side and onto the saddle along-side some spinelike boulders. Through the windows between them, we saw the view to the west and felt the strong blasts of wind up Seventy-five Mile Canyon. Wind and rain had carved this rocky backbone. One day it would be gone, but for now Esther proposed calling it the "stegosaurus rocks," after the dinosaur with bony plates along its back. (Jim later told me that the locals call it that, too.)

After the rocks, we came to a small clearing at the end of the saddle. Scattered around it were junipers stunted from the harsh winds and the thin soil. We took a break on the quiet Tanner side of the saddle and listened to the low whooing of the wind way to the east, up the east arm of Tanner Canyon. We were in a place of calm between two windy canyons.

We decided to cache our extra water here for tomorrow, because we knew we'd remember this clearing. We tucked our con-tainers in separate places among rocks and junipers, seeking to hide them as much from other humans as from rodents. It is a sad fact that you can't always trust your neighbor to leave your life-support-ing water for you. On the other hand, we found an empty container hanging from a mesquite tree at Tanner Beach, left for others by a thoughtful hiker who didn't need it. Intact, empty water containers are not to be considered litter in the Grand Canyon!

From the cairn-marked continuation of the trail, we sighted the line to our caches, jotting notes of conspicuous features that would also point us to them. Then we began a rolling 3-mile traverse down through the rest of the Supai Group, first northeast-then-north around Escalante Butte, then northeast-then-north around Cardenas, with one or two major ups and downs. The 1962 map shows the old route around Cardenas, about 150 feet higher than the present route.

The Supai went on endlessly, but the trail was clear and not very rubbly, and it afforded fast walking. It was unexposed, staying along the sides of the buttes, with rounded, boulder-strewn hills and terraces rolling outward for a quarter of a mile and ending at the top of the Redwall cliff in the west arm of Tanner Canyon. Somewhere out on those terraces, Jim told me, he found remnants of what may have been a corral where the horsethieves changed the brands of their stolen mounts.

Sparse pinyons and junipers offered bits of shade. We passed a lot of dead junipers, too, and mats of white phlox, red Indian paintbrush, grizzly bear cactus (fuzzier, spinier relatives of the prickly pear), the last of the buffaloberry, and some patches of cryptogamic soil. The Watchtower at Desert View stayed in sight, along with the massive Palisades.

Eventually we turned our backs on the Watchtower and climbed north around the east side of Cardenas Butte. Then we moved downward on our final approach to the break for the Redwall and had a teaser view of the river and the Canyon to the north.

Across Tanner Canyon, the Palisades were becoming something felt as well as seen. All the formations from the Tapeats Sandstone to the Kaibab Limestone were stacked in a nearly vertical wall 3000 feet high that was scooped with deep bays of sheer Redwall Limestone. The Redwall over there was several hundred feet lower than the Redwall here, dropped by the Butte Fault, which runs up Tanner Canyon. Below the Tapeats, at the seam of the Great Unconformity, was the Dox Sandstone, in purple-red and brick-red shaley sandstone cliffs and steep taluses fanning out to the floor of Tanner Canyon and the river.

The Palisades ran from the head of Tanner Canyon (east arm) out towards the river and up to the mouth of the Little Colorado River. From there, the cliffs extended up the Colorado another 10 miles and were known in that segment as the Desert Facade. They were a constant, palpable presence, and we always heard the wind churning along them in Tanner Canyon.

We reached the break for the Redwall descent and stopped. Rocks blocked an old trail that led straight ahead up a small rise. Our trail turned right. Esther and I looked at the faint old trail.

The Watchtower at Desert View, seen from the south flank of Cardenas Butte

It was only late morning. We'd come about halfway (we'd later realize that this had been the shorter half!). We weren't in a hurry, and we were curious. We went straight ahead up the rise. In 100 yards we came to a spectacular overlook. We dropped our packs and took a long break here, because this was a good place to just sit and look.

It was a breathtaking scene of space and floating color under dazzling light, the very opposite of Bass Canyon's brooding closeness in 1983. The Canyon opened wide to the north in a vast rimmed bowl painted in pinks, reds, purples, grays, greens, and ocher. The blue sky was gap-toothed with pinnacles and buttes. The Colorado River flowed emerald green 2700 feet below, languidly curving past gentle red hills and sharp greenish-black cliffs and broad, white, rock-strewn beaches.

Directly across the river from us was Basalt Canyon, named for its charcoal-gray walls of Cardenas Lavas, a member of the Grand Canyon Supergroup resting on top of the Dox Sandstone. In places, white salt leached from the lava walls. Other formations above the Cardenas and extending north in the Canyon were members of the Chuar Group, a subgroup of the Grand Canyon Supergroup found only in this part of the Grand Canyon and only here on the entire planet. In the unnamed canyon just to our left was more of the Cardenas Lavas, far below us between the Tapeats and the Dox.

Across the unnamed canyon, on top of the Redwall toward its north end, we saw a natural arch. We'd also be able to see it from the trail along the ridgeline traverse of the Tapeats Sandstone. And behind us, though we didn't know about it then, was a feature Jim later pointed out to me, a window way up in a fin of the Kaibab Limestone to the east of Desert View. It can be seen from the Redwall overlook where we sat and from the trail, starting near the Redwall descent and all the way down to the Tapeats and for a half mile or so below. You have to look for it, and since we didn't know about it, Esther and I never saw it.

It was a lot to take in at once. I remembered what a park service ranger once said to me: "The Grand Canyon is first and foremost a lesson in geology." Not everyone might agree, but as a layman I certainly did. Like Harvey Butchart, I tried to pick up some new lesson in geology or other natural science on every trip. Harvey said, "The great outdoors is a friendlier place if one knows the names of things." Maybe that was the final answer to my musings on why

I liked to learn the names of things: names were a starting point for the learning and understanding that helped make the Grand Canyon a friendlier and ever more wonder-filled place for me.

Names also helped me to organize what I was looking at. That big slanting butte at the right end of the panorama, for instance, was Chuar Butte, where the airplanes went down. On my first river trip here in 1973, I'd seen pieces of metal on its flanks, glinting in the sunlight. This was before the efforts, in 1976, to remove by helicopter as many of the remaining pieces as possible from such forbidding terrain. Far in the distance east of Siegfried Pyre was an unnamed peak shown as elevation 7605 feet on the map. It may someday be named after Harvey Butchart, and I like that idea; it'd get my vote.

Names could label and explain the Canyon's elements, but they couldn't describe the brilliant spectacle before us. On the more mundane scale of things, Esther said her feet were hot. She took off her boots and socks and wetted her feet with water. It looked so refreshing, I did the same. We slathered on sunscreen and lounged there against our packs, barefoot and still, warmed by the sun and soothed by soft breezes, surrounded by space and color and light. We daydreamed. We drank. We ate lunch. And we left at noon.

The trail turned east and descended the Redwall in moderately rocky, scree-y switchbacks. This passage of the Redwall was unusual in the Grand Canyon because it wasn't hacked out of an eroded vertical wall. It was on an open, slumped, and broken cliff that one could clamber up or down without the aid of switchbacks, if one had to. Not so, those implacable cliffs across the way! My eyes scanned them and continually returned to the tall headland with the column below it: Comanche Point. The sound of the name rang right, sounding like "commanding," which the point clearly was. (Names again.)

We passed to the right of a small clearing and continued downward, heading into the Muav Limestone. The trail went east and then north, switchbacking and then traversing steeply down through the Muav, which was mostly covered by talus. Boulders were scattered all around, poised to continue their transit to the river and to end up trapped behind Hoover Dam in Lake Mead 200 miles downstream. The trail was a mess of rubble cutting across the jumbled slope. We looked down at, and eventually passed alongside the base of, an outcrop of the Muav, a small turreted cliff in pale greens and ochers that looked very much like the Bright Angel Shale. Jim later explained that the Muav and Bright Angel Shale "intertongue," or interweave with one another, as do the Bright Angel and the Tapeats Sandstone. Thus, the similarities – and the confusion. Altogether, the three formations are known as the Tonto Group.

We were well below the usual range for members of the pinyon-juniper community, but after the turreted Muav cliff, the trail crossed the head of a northeast-facing ravine that was just cool and shady enough to support a small woodland niche of serviceberry bushes, pungent, pale hoptrees, and some juniper trees, mingling with the desert plants. After the ravine, we skittered across a short, nasty little ledge in the Bright Angel Shale and were now back in the exclusive company of desert scrub and grasses and small, short-stemmed yellow flowers called draba, which were almost done flowering and which were everywhere.

The river and Chuar Butte were always in view as we continued north down through the Bright Angel Shale and came onto a small saddle about 1000 feet directly below our Redwall overlook rest stop. Once again the Canyon opened up, giving a sweeping view west to east and an up-close look at the Cardenas Lavas cliff in the unnamed canyon on our left. A group of hikers on their way up was resting here. Some of them looked demoralized. When we asked how their hike was going, one just shook his head, looked forlornly down the trail and then back at us and said, "It's so long and steep."

Onward, northward, steeply downward in the Bright Angel. Here and there a clump of barrel cactus, an agave with a maturing shoot, locoweed forming its purple-speckled, ground-hugging pods, grizzly bear cactus flowering, draba blooms finishing. Behind us, the Watchtower. *Out there*, the Palisades and the wind up Tanner Canyon. The trail followed the ridgeline and was reasonably smooth and pleasantly breezy. It entered the Tapeats Sandstone, moving steeply still, down more bouldery slopes. Some of the rocks had green lichen on them; they might not have moved in a thousand or more years.

I was oohing and ahing, taking pictures of cactus flowers, and generally being my normal excitable self. "Esther, look at this! Esther, come see!" But I noticed her enthusiasm was waning.

"What's wrong?" I asked.

"My feet are burning," she said.

"Hang in there," I said. "The river's in view and we're getting closer to it."

We were, but not as fast as we thought. Below the Redwall, the Tanner Trail begins to stretch longer the farther you travel on it. It's so open, the distances are deceptive. In the heat of summer, under the roaring fireball of the sun, this part of the hike would feel like one of those dreams where you're trying to move but can't seem to get anywhere.

Now we passed the Great Unconformity and entered the Dox Sandstone. We'd be in it, heading north, all the way to the beach. The Dox is the most massive formation in the Grand Canyon, attaining thicknesses up to 3175 feet, most of it in slanting beds deep below river level. About 1200 feet of it was exposed here. That is, we were still a good 1200 feet above the river, and about 1.5 miles from Tanner Beach.

The vivid brick-red hills were liberally sprinkled with desert scrub and cactus and now flaxen grasses and brittlebushes with their yellow flowers. We descended steeply on tight, shaley gravel that was a good walking surface for lug-soled boots. In some places, however, the trail had been pounded to dust by travelers, and in these merci-fully brief stretches it made for dunelike travail. So punishingly hot are the red Dox hills in summer that river runners call this section of the Canyon "Furnace Flats."

I stopped to take a picture. "Esther, how come you're not taking any pictures?" I asked.

"Because if I stop moving I'm going to cut my feet off instead," she joked. I put my camera away, so we could keep moving.

And now we came to the most delightful part of the Dox descent. If the trail had been relentlessly steep up till now, the next 0.2 miles beat all. The trail went downhill at an *incredibly* sharp angle. Jim calls this stretch "Asinine Hill," because it is asinine for the trail not to switchback down it. (The hill across from Ribbon Falls on the North Kaibab Trail is also called "Asinine Hill" by the locals.)

Below Asinine Hill we looked down at the floor of Tanner Canyon for a while; then the trail took us away from it; then back to it. The trail went downhill for a while, then contoured, then downhill. The Dox just went on and on. We saw the greenish-black cliff of basaltic Cardenas Lavas across from Tanner Beach (it looked like a moldy haunted castle), and we saw and heard the river. But neither seemed to get any closer.

Then, in the last quarter of a mile, the trail passed some dipping slabs of the Dox and came down to the broad, gravelly creek floor. Cairns directed us into the main bed. As we walked down it, we looked back several times to make note of where the cairns were, for our return.

Finally, we saw the river dead ahead through the mesquite and tamarisk. We made for the rocks at its edge. Esther took off her boots and socks and cooled her hot, battered feet in the river. They weren't blistered; they were just sore.

It was four o'clock. We'd been on the trail since 8 A.M. We'd taken our time, drunk more than a gallon of water each, eaten and rested often, and taken a couple of long, luxurious breaks. We were in good shape, even though our feet were hot and sore. They'd be fine tomorrow. Still, we regretted having to leave so soon. We would have liked to stay a day to rest, watch the river, explore the beach, maybe hike a bit on the Escalante and Beamer routes.

The beach was quite large and dune-y, and other parties were camped on it, well out of sight and sound of one another. We camped on a dune on the west side of the creekbed under a mesquite tree that was so ancient the dune had engulfed its massive, gnarled trunk up to the first tier of branches. The branches radiated from the trunk like swollen spider's legs, meeting the ground again ten feet away. There was ample space for bedrolls between them. After dinner, we tossed cords over a branch on the second tier and suspended our packs and food from them, eight feet above the ground. Then we went down to the river to sit.

Here among the rocks at the river's edge, spindly antennas of tamarisk probed the air, bearing witness to the great shearing flows released from Glen Canyon Dam in 1983. Sweetly fragrant white sand verbenas unfolded their clusters of day-shy blossoms and delicately perfumed the balmy air.

In front of us was Tanner Rapids. Across the rapids was the gloomy, elemental green-black cliff of Cardenas Lavas that we'd seen from the trail. Now we could also see that its streamers of scree were dotted with brittlebushes finishing up their blooms. The bright yellow flowers lent an incongruous cheeriness to the House-of-Usher rock.

There was something else, too: the cliff was flanked by red Dox terraces. It was a graben, a depressed area between two faults, meaning that the whole lava cliff had dropped lower than the red strata on either side of it.

But now it was time to be done with naming things. Esther and I sat quietly, letting sunset come, letting the rock, the river, the sand, and the sweet scented air enter us, until we felt we could dissolve and flow back out into them. At dusk we returned to camp and got into our sleeping bags. We watched the stars come out and erase the moonless sky. We fell asleep, lulled by the sound of the rapids.

April 30

Before we left, I took a brief hike up the dune above us, just to have a look. The sand held patches of orange globe mallows and white evening primroses mixed in with grasses. A rattlesnake had left a sinuous groove that went from a hole under one bush to another bush twenty feet away, crossing a freeway interchange of toad and lizard tracks. Part of Vishnu Temple's peak was visible downriver. Across the creekbed, several canyon wrens were having a morning's coffee klatch, employing a more diverse vocabulary than I'd ever heard them use before. Everything was complete in this moment, yet there was also prologue and promise.

We set out at seven o'clock – late by Grand Canyon standards, especially if this had been in summer – and again the Tanner Trail earned its reputation: it was punishingly, endlessly long and steep. More than ever before, my Ex-hale-In-hale-Two-step served me. It didn't just help me to climb. It became a backdrop to my thoughts, an oceanlike "white noise" that freed my consciousness to appreciate what was around me.[1] At the same time, on another level of consciousness, I knew that my rhythmic breathing connected me to Canyon rhythms that I couldn't perceive through my senses. I rejoiced in that mysterious connection, in the midst of my discomfort.

I followed strong, easy-striding Esther up the hill, breathing Ex(step) . . . hale(step) . . . In(step) . . . hale(step). . . . We climb-contour-climbed the Dox, looking across the way at its red taluses and cliffs. We leaned against Asinine Hill every forty-five seconds to rest, until we were done with it—ten minutes of agony.

The Watchtower was nearly always in view, and as the river had done yesterday, the Tower came to represent our always-there-not-getting-any-closer destination. We heard the low roar of the wind up Tanner Canyon, a sound like the river. And we felt the stupefying presence of those magnificent, impossible cliffs of the Palisades of the Desert. We watched warily as the sun rose above them, getting ready for its day-long blitz on the desert, and we were grateful to be doing this trek before summer.

On top of the Tapeats we looked at the basaltic Cardenas cliffs in the unnamed canyon on our right—green-black and sheer. We climbed the jumbled, draba-dotted slopes of the Bright Angel Shale and passed the odorous hoptrees in the ravine. Ex . . . hale . . . In . . . hale. . . . So steep. So interminably long. We sweated; we rested and drank.

We skirted the base of the turreted Muav Limestone cliff and labored up the cruel slopes of the Muav. Red penstemon flowering here; that colossal, indifferent presence across the way, and the never-ceasing shooing of the wind up Tanner Canyon. Overhead, a hawk chased a glossy-winged raven and sent it packing. It was the first time I'd ever heard a raven "cry Uncle."

We took a long break on the clearing near the base of the Redwall. Then up the Redwall, Ex . . . hale . . . In . . . hale. . . , pausing every two to five minutes to ease leg aches. We made it in one hour and celebrated with another rest. The great barrier was passed. Now we were in pinyon-juniper country, albeit rather sparse here on the Supai flank of Cardenas Butte. Still, it felt like home. Even the Watchtower appeared larger—and closer, at last! We paced ourselves in the rolling 3-mile traverse up the Supai Group, so as not to burn out before the last upward pull. I let my breathing come in three-steps, and finally just let it breathe itself. Done with Cardenas Butte, coming around Escalante. Here were our patches of cryptogam, and the buffaloberry began: little landmarks to cheer us on our way.

We retrieved our water caches at the clearing at Seventy-five Mile Saddle and had a break, listening to the wind far away in the east arm of Tanner Canyon. Then we started again, passing behind the stegosaurus rocks like duck decoys at an amusement park arcade. Now the coyote droppings and lichens. Ex . . . hale . . . In . . . hale . . . , up the Hermit Shale, the Coconino Sandstone, the Toroweap Formation, and the Kaibab Limestone. Steep, achingly steep, but cool in the shelter of the Douglas firs.

At three-thirty we were out—but not done. Having flown to the Grand Canyon, Esther and I had had to take a taxi to the trailhead. Now we had to walk to Desert View to telephone for a ride back to the Village. So it was another 0.4 miles out the spur road to the East Rim Drive and then 2 miles east on the Drive—uphill, of course!—to Desert View.

As we trudged up the road, I suddenly became aware that I had just completed hiking all the main trails of the South Rim of the Grand Canyon. Tired as I was, I was elated. I realized I'd come a long way as a hiker since our first faltering trek on the Hermit Trail in 1979. And I knew I wasn't done hiking in the Grand Canyon. Our Boucher-Slate trip with Bob was coming up, and after that, well, who knew what. The point was, I'd keep coming back. No matter how long or punishing the trail, the Canyon kept luring me back.

We made our call at Desert View and walked past the Watchtower to the rim. The Tower stood barely twenty yards behind us now. Off to our right was the rippling rampart of the Palisades of the Desert. Out there, in the middle of an S-curve of the river, was Tanner Beach, with the lava graben across from it, 9 miles and 4600 feet from the trailhead. And beyond, in long, slanting late-afternoon light and shadow, was the vast rimmed bowl with its whipped rainbow meringue of canyons, peaks, and buttes.

It's always a bit mind-boggling, at the end of a Grand Canyon hike, to look back at where you've just been. It's also a bit mind-bending to contemplate the parade of humanity that traveled the route before you. The Tanner Trail has been used for over 800 years, first by Indians who farmed the creek bottoms across the river at Unkar and Nankoweap, then by their descendants who used it in pilgrimage to their religious shrines, and more recently by white men seeking access to mines, clandestine corrals, and buried treasures. All of them toiled along the Tanner Trail for their livelihoods, sacred and profane. Today, people toil on this and all the other trails in the Grand Canyon for recreation — literally, to refresh and recreate themselves in body and spirit.

The taxi arrived at five-thirty. We reached our lodging at six-thirty and found Bob waiting for us. We called the BRO to check in and went immediately to the restaurant to celebrate.

Notes

1. Paying attention to what's around you while hiking in the Grand Canyon often is an intermittent business, because you're constantly having to watch your footing. This is true even for experts. Harvey Butchart told me, "There have been times when I was watching my footing so constantly that I walked right by prime items. I once walked from the mouth of the Little Colorado to the Hopis' Salt Trail Canyon, mostly on the south side, without noticing the Sipapu across the river." Jim Ohlman told me, "I have pulled this very same stunt twice in one trip, but I have seen the Sipapu twice since then, and it is sort of like missing a red Cadillac parked in your living room!" If you want to *see*, you need to stop and rest.

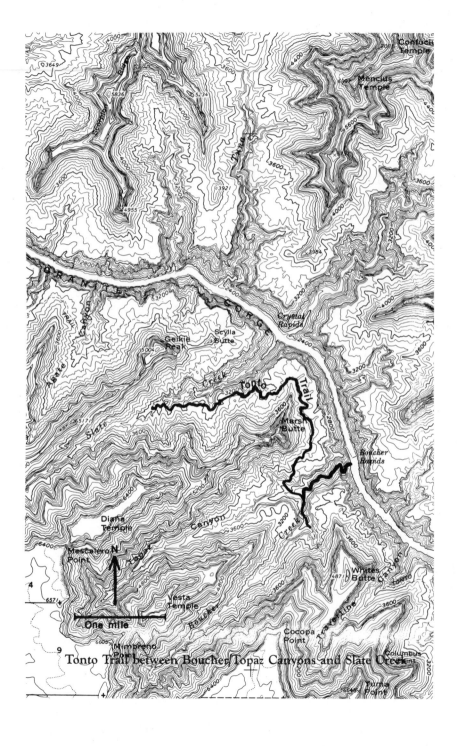

Tonto Trail between Boucher-Topaz Canyons and Slate Creek

CHAPTER 8

With People and Alone, 1984/1986
(To the Memory of Steve)

Until now, Bob and I had seldom seen more than a few other hikers along the unmaintained trails in the Grand Canyon. Maybe it was coincidence, or maybe it was the season or the increasing popularity of the Boucher-Hermit area since our trip in 1982, but on our five-day, 39-mile[1] Boucher hike with Esther we encountered a number of hikers. Some of them were funny or merely eccentric, but one suffered serious misfortune.

May 2

Right off the bat, at Hermits Rest, we met three hikers bound for Hermit Rapids whose leader was an unforgettable fellow I later named "Mr. Bean'n'Bauer." Mr. Bean'n'Bauer was wearing or carrying every conceivable item of first-class, high-tech, mail-order-catalog gear: camouflage-print trousers and shirt loaded with pockets and loops, safari hat, pedometer, altimeter, binoculars, cameras with lenses and filters, map case, and whatallelse inside his pockets and backpack, besides water and food.

Bean'n'Bauer was an unabashed outdoors-gear and Grand Canyon fanatic, a pleasant and otherwise normal-seeming fellow. He told us he didn't mind carrying all that extra weight. For him it was part of the fun of the "expedition." He was all the more remarkable because one of his legs was bad and he gamely trod the Canyon's difficult terrain with a pronounced limp. Surprisingly, he used not a spiffy new L. L. Bean or Eddie Bauer walking staff, but a heavy,

Utah agaves in bloom near mouth of Boucher Creek

old-fashioned mahogany cane. He may have looked a little absurd, but he had grit and dignity, and he was broadly experienced in the Grand Canyon backcountry.

He was leading his two routinely-decked-out buddies into the Canyon for their first time. They both claimed to have done a lot of hiking in the mountains of California, but early on one of them showed a lack of familiarity with wilderness etiquette, cutting across switchbacks. To Bean'n'Bauer's credit, he told his buddy to stop cutting switchbacks because it hastens erosion. There was also a lot of initial shaking-down going on among them – changing clothes, adjusting laces and straps, rehanging gadgets and gismos – and we quickly left them well behind.

In Hermit Basin we encountered another trio, two men and a woman, heading for Boucher Creek and, via the Tonto Trail, Bass Canyon. They were planning to meet some friends doing this trip from the opposite direction and to exchange car keys for transportation at each end. They didn't seem to know much about Grand Canyon hiking. Their car key connection was going to be chancy, as the Tonto is obscure or in divergent tracks west of Slate Canyon. They might miss their friends altogether. In addition, they were oddly provisioned, carrying fresh bacon and as much bourbon as water. Later in the day, on a break, we saw the men half-carrying the woman. The exposures and steep descents of the Boucher Trail can defeat the spirits, knees, and feet of the beginner.

Even Esther said she had a touch of acrophobia on the narrow, scary ledges on top of the Supai coming up to the head of Travertine Canyon from Yuma Point.[2] Fortunately, those stretches are few and brief, and we had an otherwise smooth trip all 11 miles to Boucher Rapids, arriving in time to photograph two flowering agaves on a sandy platform in the Vishnu Schist at the mouth of the creek. We caught them at the perfect moment when they were dazzlingly backlit by the late afternoon sun.

The beach at Boucher Rapids was clean and white, and we camped on a wind-sheltered spot behind a boulder on the east side of the creek.

May 3

We awoke to find toad prints and lizard tracks in the sand all around our ground cloths. This is usual on the beaches. They come to inspect campers while they sleep. We spent time in the morning just sitting in solitary reveries before the light-spangled rapids, a quarter mile of dance and glitter. Two ravens played back and forth across the faceted waters, and I wished I could be one of them, seeing what they saw, feeling the spray and the air currents and learning something of the raven's mood for play.

We headed up Boucher Canyon and found the cairn-marked continuation of the Tonto Trail on the west side of Topaz Canyon just at its junction with Boucher Canyon. We climbed up onto the Tonto Plateau and walked 5 easy miles across a checkerboard of blackbrush and gorgeously flowering *Opuntia* (the genus encompassing the prickly pear and grizzly bear cactus). Their blossoms were large, with luscious, translucent petals in salmons and pinks and lavenders and every hue in between. As fabulous as they were, they were only the first flowers of spring. Each plant had many more buds than it had open blossoms.

Across the Gorge, long, sheer fingers of Redwall Limestone reached out from the Tower of Ra and cut deeply back into it in gigantic amphitheaters. The great red walls moved along with us, seeming to slide past one another like panels in a Japanese teahouse. We had a good view of Scylla Butte across Slate Canyon. It was a small tower of Bright Angel Shale capped with Muav Limestone that so far had resisted erosion.

We met a short, compact man coming east who'd been hiking alone on the north side for a month. He had paddled across the river at W. W. Bass's Shinumo crossing in a little inflatable raft he was carrying. He moved slowly; he was mellowed and completely plugged into the Canyon's rhythms. He had turned the colors of the Canyon. His bare chest was tanned to a rich golden brown, and his hair and beard were sunbleached a honeyed bronze. His navy shorts were smudged and stained red from the shales. His worn backpack was faded gray-green like the Tonto scrub; and his eyes were intensely blue like the sky, in eyeballs shot with veins as pink as Zoroaster Granite from so many days in the glare of the desert. We asked him if he'd seen any people on the north side.

"I was off the trails," he said with a smile. "I didn't see anyone till I got onto the Tonto past Bass Canyon. It's taken me a while to get used to talking again."

"What did you do about water and food for a month?" we asked.

"I brought in caches before I started."

"Did you see a lot of Indian ruins?"

He smiled again and looked into the distance. "Yes, I did," he said in his soft, slow way, seeming to commune with an inner source.

"Speaking of ruins," I said, "did you happen to see a three-some—two men and a woman—between here and Bass? She was having trouble with her feet."

"No, I didn't see them," he said, "but the Tonto's sort of vague west of here. I might've missed them."

"Where're you headed now?" Bob asked.

"Out . . . one way or another." He shrugged lightly, looked into the distance again and then back at us, and ran his fingers through his hair. "Maybe Boucher, maybe Hermit. I don't think I'm ready for all the pilgrims on the Bright Angel."

We laughed. We understood. He was trying to delay his re-entry shock. We would have liked to learn more about him and his travels, but we respected his effort to make a gradual return to society. So we wished him well and continued on our way. But some paces beyond, Bob and Esther and I turned and looked back, to make sure we'd really met this traveler. He was there, all right, moving slowly. He blended with the Canyon. It had hardened his body but made him quiet inside, and that quiet lent him an aura of other-worldliness that we could almost feel. It was as though he had stepped out of a time warp to remind us of the Canyon's mystery and its power to change those who venture into it.

On we went. As we approached Slate Canyon, the black Vishnu Schist across the Inner Gorge became broadly banded with an erratic fretwork of Zoroaster Granite. I recognized this wall from my river trips: below it was Crystal Rapids, mile 98. We couldn't see or hear the river from here. I strode out between the blackbrush and the cactus for a distance toward the river, until I could hear Crystal thrashing around down there like an angry, caged tiger.

Crystal is a monster rapids, formed overnight by the same thousand-year flood that tore out the transcanyon pipeline and the bridges on the North Kaibab Trail in Bright Angel Canyon in December 1966. Mountains of rock roared down the Dragon and Crystal drainages at speeds estimated up to fifty miles per hour and dumped room-sized boulders into the river. Anasazi ruins located a good twenty feet above normal creek level were carried away.

Crystal's delta enlarged fourfold, and what had been a modest rapids now was a raging maelstrom with a gaping, seething hole on the south side, another menacing boulder downstream, and tailwaves that disappear around a bend a half mile beyond.[3]

Crystal Rapids was the reason for our trek to Slate Canyon. We hoped to get down Slate the 2 miles or so to see Crystal. The BRO had said it was possible but didn't tell us that there were two falls to bypass. When we reached Slate Canyon, Bob reconnoitered down Slate while Esther and I filled our bottles (there were still a few pools and a trickle of flow in the creekbed).

Bob was gone a long time. When he returned he said he had been unable to go down the bed. He had come to a fall and found a good trail going west around it and back into the bed below it. Then the walls had narrowed and he came to the lip of another, higher fall. No bypass here: the walls were too steep. Bob considered it too risky to try to go down the fall without a rope and a companion. He might be unable to climb back up. So he spent an hour at the lip – a trickle of water was going over the fall – enjoying the profound solitude of the spot, then returned. We were disappointed not to be able to reach Crystal, but the walk over to Slate had been worthwhile, just to see the glorious cactus flowers and those marvelous, gigantic, scalloped red walls across the Gorge.

You *can* get down Slate Canyon. Jim Ohlman told us how, and we hope to go back someday and do it:

"First you get into the bed of Slate Canyon. You can start where the Tonto Trail meets Slate, scrambling down ledges in the bed. Or, if you're coming over from Boucher, you can save yourself some backtracking by entering Slate Canyon at a ravine just to the east of a 'finger' (that's what it looks like on the map) of Tapeats Sandstone that's about an eighth of a mile east of the junction of the Tonto Trail with Slate Canyon. This finger is right along the 3200-foot contour line on the map. You scramble down the ravine (the route's unmarked) on the east side of the finger.

"Once you're in the bed, you come to a place where the bed meanders west. The first fall is about midway along this meander – that is, at its west-most extreme – and the second fall is near its return (east end). *Avoid entering the meander.* Above you on the east side of the bed is a column of Tapeats, standing free of the Tapeats rim on the east. You clamber up over the saddle between the column and the east rim, and scramble steeply down the north side, ending back in the bed below the falls. From there on there's only occasional scrambling in the bed, all the way to the river."

We spent the night at Slate Canyon. Two hikers arrived in early evening, on their way back from hiking farther west on the Tonto. They had a loose, unorganized aspect, looking more like caricatures of hikers than the real thing. Between them they were getting by on only six quarts of water a day—here on the Tonto with temperatures already in the eighties! Each carried a quart canteen, and they took turns lugging a water-filled, gallon-size juice jug that leaked. They played practical jokes on one another. One had filled the other's pack with rocks when the latter went off to relieve himself. We asked them if they'd seen the bacon-and-booze trio. They had and said the woman seemed to be managing. At least, she was now able to carry her own pack. We talked awhile longer, and they went off to camp downcanyon.

May 4

We reached Hermit Creek—11 miles—by 1 P.M., bleary-eyed and dazed. We claimed the Dormitory, then hung our packs from cords we tossed over the pack bar. At last we were able to enjoy ourselves at Hermit, free from concern about rodents. A perky little canyon wren, an unremarkable brown with a white breast and brown belly, was our mascot at the Dormitory, hopping around and eating ants while we were there, but never giving its call.

Esther and I went to the pool. We were having a quiet conversation when two men and a woman came down. One of the men, a short, stocky, hairy fellow, took off every bit of clothing except his two elastic knee braces. The unexpected and unavoidable sight of soft pink flesh surrounded by sweat-coiled black hair undid my concentration and stopped me in mid-sentence. Esther said she'd never seen me look so dumbfounded. We barely stifled our laughter.

May 5

With our packs hanging from the pack bar, we went to Hermit Rapids. We had it to ourselves. The water was green. We rested under some tamarisk at the creek (after checking first for scorpions). An hour later, the river had turned brown and risen a foot. We looked at the river and then at one another.

"You don't suppose the dam . . .?"

"Naw. We'd be warned in plenty of time . . . I think."

Glen Canyon Dam is leaky and is widely hated, and everyone from scientists to angry laymen has personal estimates on how long it will take to silt up completely or break apart—anywhere from 60 to 300 years. The dam was intact today. Although the weather was flawless here, there'd been rain in drainages somewhere upstream. That had colored the water, and the dam's releases accounted for the river's rise.

On our way back from the rapids, a scant 100 yards from camp, we came upon the aftermath of a near-fatal accident. A young man had just fallen down a forty-foot "chimney," a dry fall in the Tapeats in an alcove in the wall of Hermit Canyon. He was conscious, but both his feet and ankles were broken and badly misshapen. He was only nineteen years old, and this was his first trip in the Grand Canyon. His companion, a man in his mid-twenties, had hiked here before and had suggested they take this "shortcut" down to the creek from the top of the Tapeats (Tonto Plateau) above. The young man had said he'd prefer not to, that he wasn't a climber and would just as soon stay on the trail. But peer pressure overruled his good judgment. He'd lost his grip and had slid to the floor, and here he was, eyes glazed, his twisted and swollen feet dangling in the cool stream, where he'd been moved to help control swelling.

Attending him was a doctor who fortunately happened to be camping at Hermit with his wife and teenaged son. He treated the young man to prevent shock—kept him reclining; kept his body temperature constant by covering him with a light wrap in this cool, shady place; talked reassuringly to him; and, since the young man was conscious, encouraged him to sip fluids. When the young man had stabilized, the doctor gave him some codeine for pain.

Two hikers came by who said they were leaving for the rim at around three o'clock and would go for help. Meanwhile, we tried to attract aid with signal mirrors. Bob fetched a large mirror and went up to the (unmanned) ranger cabin on the Tonto Plateau. I used a smaller mirror from the Dormitory. Until sunset, we signaled to the rim and at every passing aircraft. When we checked in at the BRO after our trip, we were told that our flashes had been seen on the rim but not by aircraft, and that no one who'd seen the flashes had thought anything of them at the time. So much for this time-honored method of summoning help!

We checked on the young man off and on that evening. He'd been carefully moved away from the stream and placed in a light sleeping bag. He was dry, drugged, and reasonably comfortable. The doctor told us privately that the breaks appeared to be so severe—one heel appeared crushed—that the young man probably would need surgery and long-term physical therapy afterward. "I doubt he'll ever hike or play active sports again," the doctor said.

We never learned the doctor's medical specialty and had fun speculating that he was a gynecologist or dermatologist. He was a smoker, and he shambled around camp in sneakers. He and his family had come over from Boucher Creek, and he said his descent of the Boucher Trail had been his "Day of Terror."

May 6

With no moon to hike by, we started at dawn. By six-thirty, when we were up in the Muav, we saw a helicopter heading into Hermit Gorge. It looked like a little orange bean down there. Its rotors fluttered loudly in the sheer-walled gorge. It landed just above the camp and, so we were told later, its crew took a litter down the trail to carry the young man back up to the helicopter.

For my part, I found myself inexplicably crying as I moved up the trail, and I asked Esther and Bob to go on ahead of me and let me hike alone. Bob was concerned and didn't want to leave me, but I assured him I was okay. I just needed to cry and be alone, though at the time I didn't know why I was crying.

As I sobbed and staggered up the trail (I discovered it's nearly impossible to cry and climb at the same time), I found myself looking again and again at the bays of Redwall across Hermit Gorge. Eventually, I began to "see" a figure in one of them and me in one next to it. The figure was that of my dear friend Steve Green, who had died of a rare heart infection three months before, at only forty-one. He'd been a good, loyal friend since we'd met in college. Steve had been the unwitting igniter of my passion for the Grand Canyon, having organized the group that went on my first river trip here in 1973.

Since he'd died, I hadn't been able to cry for him. I thought about him often, but the tears wouldn't come. Now, at last, they came. They flowed and overflowed. Those twin bays in the Redwall seemed to represent our connected lives, and they released memories of our twenty-year friendship. As I glutted myself on the spring-time sights and scents along the trail and stared into those red bays and wailed, I felt as though I was imbibing Steve's presence.

Bob and Esther were waiting for me at Santa Maria Spring. I was about cried-out by then. We hiked together, now, bringing our faces close to the flowers, sniffing our way up the spring-fresh trail. In a ravine high in the Supai, just below Hermit Basin, we came upon a redbud tree in an explosion of pink and purple bloom; its leaves would come out later. Although we had almost 2 miles and a good 1500 feet to go, that redbud tree was for me the climax of the hike out and an affirmation and celebration of Steve's life, of all life. I was unpent and spent and glad my grief had "waited" for this special place and time.

Sometimes the Canyon does things like this to you.

Back in Denver that summer, one of the men at Bob's office said, "Gee, you're lucky your wife goes with you on those backpack trips in the Grand Canyon."

"You have it backwards," Bob said. "Sharon makes all the plans. I go to keep her company."

But not this time. I decided to hike one solo.

Ever since we'd met the woman hiking the Hermit and the Tanner alone in 1982, I'd had the idea I might one day do a solo in the Canyon myself. It was a personal challenge I wanted to meet. I was curious about how I would like going it alone. Now I felt ready to try it.

I hiked in September for three days: down the Bright Angel Trail to Indian Gardens, then west across the Tonto to Hermit Creek, and out the Hermit Trail, for a total of about 26 miles, with overnights at Horn Creek and Hermit.

September 12

The Bright Angel Trail was an *autobahn*, a German freeway.

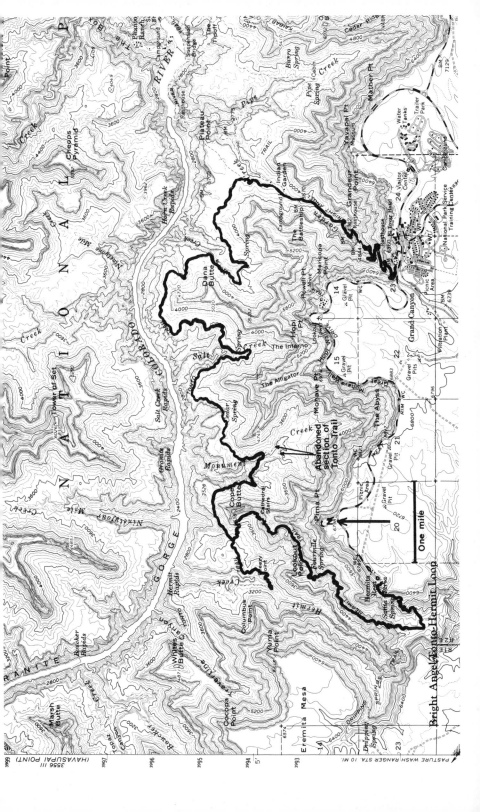

Bright Angel–Tonto–Hermit Loop

I was one of the few English-speaking people on it, all of West Germany's hikers apparently having come to the Grand Canyon in September. But when I turned left onto the Tonto Trail, I found solitude, and in the 14.2 miles to Hermit Creek I met only two parties.

I relished being alone on the Tonto. I didn't have any cosmic sensations or revelations on the mystery of life. I just heard the silence and my own breathing and felt the steady, grounding reassurance of my own step-step-foot-foot along the trail. I watched the walls across the Gorge move by me (or so it seemed) and the fair-weather clouds arrange and rearrange themselves in lofting, white, woolly billows. I let the Canyon happen all around me, without labeling anything.

I spent my first night on a large, flat boulder in Horn Creek. I felt a bit jittery at first at being all alone here, but I settled in well enough and fell asleep without much resistance. In the middle of the night, I awoke to find myself eyeball-to-eyeball with a spotted skunk, who'd come up to investigate its uninvited guest. I shone my flashlight at it, stared it down, urged, "Git!" and it got. Thank heavens!

September 13

I set out by seven-eighths moonlight at 4 A.M., scanning ahead on the rolling plateau for the familiar trough between silhouetted bushes that was the trail through the blackbrush. I strode vigorously along in the deep, dead stillness of the Grand Canyon, through a world of eerie gray, moon-drenched shapes. When daylight came, the popcorn clouds formed again, but they never blocked the sun's relentless blast on the Tonto Plateau.

Colin Fletcher observed that when you're walking on the Tonto Plateau, everything across the Gorge seems to exist as if it were "behind a huge pane of glass," while next to you towers the Redwall cliff, and far above and stepped back from it, remote, hangs the rim with the human society it hosts. You, meanwhile, walk aloof on a shelf, segregated from everything on either side. If you're not unsettled by it, as I was on Bob's and my first trip in 1979, the Tonto Plateau is a good place to trek, suspended in space and time, for mile after mile of side canyon after promontory after side canyon, in nurturing solitude. This was how it felt to me that day.

I reached Monument Creek, 8.2 miles from Horn, at around

9 A.M., having given myself liberal breaks enroute. I refilled my water bottles and rested a long time in the shade along the east wall of the gorge. There was no one here, and the only sound, other than the shishing of the stream, was the clear, cascading whistle of the canyon wren.

I set out for Hermit Creek at ten-thirty. I passed one couple along the way, and at the junction of the Tonto Trail and the Hermit Trail I met two young men who were hiking and hitchhiking around the country. Their packs were heavy with all their trip cargo, as they were trekking rim-to-rim via the Hermit, Tonto, Bright Angel, and North Kaibab trails and would resume their odyssey from the North Rim. Their boots were sadly worn, and the sole of one had pulled away from its upper and flapped as he walked. I gave them my supply of duct tape, and as they jury-rigged their boots, we had a long conversation.

We said our good-byes and I walked the final mile to Hermit Creek, arriving dazed and headachy to discover instantly that something was amiss at camp. The latrine was gone, or rather, it was there in ashes. There was no one in camp. I claimed the Dormitory with my groundcloth, hung my pack, and went down to the pool. There I found a lone hiker whom I'll call Richard.

Richard was a spare, wide-staring, taut-skinned man in his mid-thirties who told me he considered himself a friend to man. He seemed gentle and good-hearted, and he spoke softly, but I had difficulty following his lines of thought. Dazed as I was from hiking in ninety-five-degree heat, I was pretty certain it wasn't *my* logic that was short-circuiting as I listened to him. Richard was plainly disoriented and out of touch with what most people think of as reality. About one thing he was lucid, however: he told me that he'd accidentally burned down the latrine.

He had arrived at Hermit the day before and was the only person at camp. He'd been annoyed by the smell of the toilet, not understanding that that was the least of evils for this close, intensively used campground. Richard thought maybe he could partially eliminate the smell by burning the toilet paper in the pit. But he didn't realize that flammable gases are released by decomposing waste. Furthermore, the Hermit station was equipped with a special ventilation device to dry out the wastes and kill bacteria. It worked too well: Richard's match ignited a conflagration at the site, and he spent the entire time of the burn chasing flying sparks and smacking them out with his shirt, trying to keep the mesquite from catching fire as well.

Richard seemed unaware of the seriousness of what he'd done. His backcountry permit was for several nights at Hermit, and he thought he'd just stay his time and then report his "bonfire," as he termed it, when he hiked out. Naturally, he said, he expected to pay for the damage. He was out of work and, for the novelty of it, he had hitchhiked to the Canyon from the East, starting out with only three dollars; but he said he'd pay for the damage somehow. He estimated it at $1500. I figured it had to be closer to $10,000 but didn't say so. And I realized, although he seemed not to, that he might go to jail. Of this possibility I also said nothing, but I did manage to persuade him to leave the next morning to report the accident. I awoke briefly at around 3 A.M. and saw him leaving the campground.

September 14

When I checked in at the BRO, I reported my meeting with Richard and was told he was right now still with park officials. He didn't go to jail, but he was heavily fined. I later learned that only two hours before Richard had arrived at Hermit Creek, park officials and engineers had been down there to inspect the latrine and had pronounced it working well! A temporary toilet was brought in by helicopter—a dicey job, as the chopper had to hover next to the Tapeats wall while workers on the ground guided the suspended station into place. Eventually, a new dehydrating toilet was installed, with extra vents and solar powered forced air circulation to speed up evaporation from the vault. It's reported to have greatly improved the air quality at the campground.

My solo had gone well, but at the time I didn't think I'd ever choose to go by myself again. I had been mildly nervous about sleeping alone at Horn Creek—probably just the uneasiness of the first-timer. But more than anything else, I had missed having a companion with whom I could share and react to the adventure. Walking alone wasn't new to me. Bob and I often hiked at a distance from one another, enjoying the solitude. But we liked having one another nearby. It wasn't just reassuring. It was more fun. Or so I thought at the time.

I was mistaken. To my surprise, I did choose to hike alone again – in October 1986: four days, Hermit-Tonto-South Kaibab, with side trips to Granite Rapids[4] and Plateau Point and overnights at Monument Creek, Salt Creek, and Indian Gardens. That trip was altogether an experience of joy, exhilaration, and renewal. As always, I was in the Canyon's thrall, but for the first time in all our hiking here, I felt as though I'd "come home." I knew then that I wanted to return solo again, in addition to hiking with others.

But in September of 1984 I couldn't have imagined this change in how I felt. I was pleased just to have met the personal challenge of going it alone in the Grand Canyon. Solo hiking should not be lightly undertaken in the Canyon, and it had been a big challenge for me. I celebrated my success with a special dinner at a restaurant on the rim.

After dinner, I walked outside to the low stone wall at the rim. I stood there, contented and alone, under the full moon, in the soft night air that now had a hint of fall crispness in it. I saw, winking back at me, the lights of the ranger station 3000 feet below at Indian Gardens, where I'd been three days ago, and the lights at Grand Canyon Lodge 10 miles across the darkened chasm on the North Rim, where I'd never been.

I thought about the trails over there – the North Kaibab, Clear Creek, Thunder River, Nankoweap, North Bass, and Lava Falls trails. I knew I'd be back to hike on the South Rim, but now I was becoming curious to explore on the other side.

"Someday we'll go there," I said, half-aloud.

And like the solitary call of the canyon wren, my words hung for a moment on the silence . . . and then fell into the rich black void.

Notes

1. Breakdown of trip distances:

Hermits Rest-Boucher Rapids	11.0
Boucher Rapids-Tonto-west at Topaz Canyon	1.5
Topaz to Slate and back to Boucher Canyon	10.5
Boucher Canyon-Hermit Creek	5.5+
Side trip to Hermit Rapids and back	3.0
Hermit Creek-Hermits Rest	7.0
Total about	38.5+

2. Hikers planning their first Grand Canyon trek would be wise to check themselves for acrophobia—fear of being in high places—and, if they have it, forget about hiking the Canyon!

3. Crystal Rapids is vividly described in chapter 9 of *The Big Drops: Ten Legendary Rapids*, by Robert O. Collins and Roderick Nash (Sierra Club Books, San Francisco, 1978).

4. Granite Rapids is at the mouth of Monument Creek. It is reached by descending the bed of Monument Creek. If you start from Monument Camp, there are some low angle chutes and sloping bedrock to negotiate. These can be bypassed, as I did, by taking the rough, steep spur trail off the Tonto Trail on the west side of Monument Canyon, only minutes from camp. A wooden post, marked with "Monument Camp" and "Granite Camp" and directional arrows, indicates the descent. The post stands just in front of the Monument, a 130-foot-high-or-so pillar of Tapeats Sandstone sitting on a stump of Zoroaster Granite, which is the feature for which Monument Canyon is named. It takes about 45 minutes to reach the river, and when I was there cairns marked bypasses of scrambly sections in the creek bed. Hikers generally camp on the dunes on the west side of the creek, alongside the rapids, but they also use the east side, above the rapids, which is where river parties stay. The east side has grotto-like campsites cleared from a tangle of tamarisk and seep-willows. The grotto campground has charm but also is home to scorpions and ring-tail cats. Granite Rapids is powerful, and from the beach there is a fine upstream view, through tight walls of Vishnu Schist, of the small South Rim-side peak known by the locals as Little Dana Butte, which is at the end of the ridge supporting Dana Butte. A drawing of this upstream view, with some artistic license, appears in Major John Wesley Powell's journal, with the caption "Running a Rapid." It's fascinating to take a photograph of this view and compare it detail-for-detail with the artist's drawing.

The Monument in Monument Canyon.

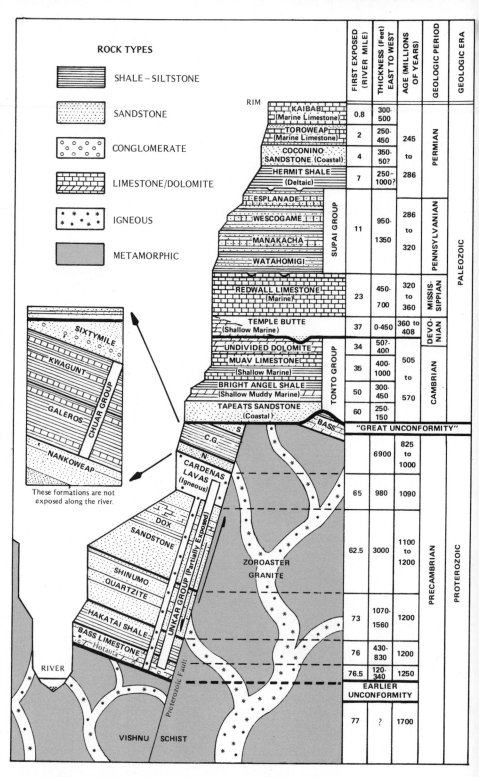

ROCK TYPES

- SHALE – SILTSTONE
- SANDSTONE
- CONGLOMERATE
- LIMESTONE/DOLOMITE
- IGNEOUS
- METAMORPHIC

RIM

	FIRST EXPOSED (RIVER MILE)	THICKNESS (Feet) EAST TO WEST	AGE (MILLIONS OF YEARS)	GEOLOGIC PERIOD	GEOLOGIC ERA
KAIBAB (Marine Limestone)	0.8	300-500		PERMIAN	
TOROWEAP (Marine Limestone)	2	250-450	245	PERMIAN	
COCONINO SANDSTONE (Coastal)	4	350-50?	to	PERMIAN	
HERMIT SHALE (Deltaic)	7	250-1000?	286	PERMIAN	PALEOZOIC
ESPLANADE / WESCOGAME / MANAKACHA / WATAHOMIGI (SUPAI GROUP)	11	950-1350	286 to 320	PENNSYLVANIAN	PALEOZOIC
REDWALL LIMESTONE (Marine)	23	450-700	320 to 360	MISSIS-SIPPIAN	PALEOZOIC
TEMPLE BUTTE (Shallow Marine)	37	0-450	360 to 408	DEVO-NIAN	PALEOZOIC
UNDIVIDED DOLOMITE	34	50?-400		CAMBRIAN	PALEOZOIC
MUAV LIMESTONE (Shallow Marine)	35	400-1000	505	CAMBRIAN	PALEOZOIC
BRIGHT ANGEL SHALE (Shallow Muddy Marine)	50	300-450	to	CAMBRIAN	PALEOZOIC
TAPEATS SANDSTONE (Coastal) (TONTO GROUP)	60	250-150	570	CAMBRIAN	PALEOZOIC

"GREAT UNCONFORMITY"

	FIRST EXPOSED	THICKNESS	AGE	GEOLOGIC PERIOD	GEOLOGIC ERA
BASS / S / C.G. / N.		6900	825 to 1000	PRECAMBRIAN	PROTEROZOIC
CARDENAS LAVAS (Igneous)	65	980	1090	PRECAMBRIAN	PROTEROZOIC
DOX SANDSTONE / ZOROASTER GRANITE (UNKAR GROUP) (Partially Exposed)	62.5	3000	1100 to 1200	PRECAMBRIAN	PROTEROZOIC
SHINUMO QUARTZITE	73	1070-1560	1200	PRECAMBRIAN	PROTEROZOIC
HAKATAI SHALE	76	430-830	1200	PRECAMBRIAN	PROTEROZOIC
BASS LIMESTONE / Hotauta	76.5	120-340	1250	PRECAMBRIAN	PROTEROZOIC

EARLIER UNCONFORMITY

VISHNU SCHIST	77	?	1700	PRECAMBRIAN	PROTEROZOIC

RIVER

Proterozoic Fault

(Inset, left)

SIXTYMILE
KWAGUNT
GALEROS
NANKOWEAP
(CHUAR GROUP)

These formations are not exposed along the river.

Paleozoic and Proterozoic Stratigraphy of Grand Canyon

APPENDIX A

Cross-section of the Rock Formations in the Grand Canyon, with Explanations

The story of the rocks of the Grand Canyon begins at the bottom of the Canyon with the dark, rugged Vishnu Schist:

Vishnu Schist: Blackish-colored metamorphic rock, often threaded with other material, including intrusions of the pink Zoroaster Granite. It erodes into massive, ragged cliffs. No life forms are found in it. About two billion years ago, the Grand Canyon region lay under a sea. Sediments were laid down to an immense thickness, with occasional volcanic activity and lava flows adding to them. Eventually they reached a thickness of 10 miles. About 1.7 billion years ago, the buried strata were buckled and folded and lifted up to form a mountain range probably as high as today's Rockies. The rocks were metamorphosed (changed in form by tremendous heat and pressure) by all these events. The mountains were eroded off to a plain over the next half billion years, and this erosional period before the deposition of later strata is known as the *Precambrian Unconformity.*

Grand Canyon Supergroup: The Vishnu plain subsided and once again was under a sea. From 1.2 to 0.8 billion years ago, two groups of sedimentary and igneous (molten, flowing) strata, the Unkar and

Note: Many thanks to Larry Stevens, author of *The Colorado River in Grand Canyon: A Guide,* for permission to reprint his chart. For more detailed but highly readable discussions of Grand Canyon geology, I recommend chapter 2 of Larry's book, part 2 of Stephen Whitney's *A Field Guide to the Grand Canyon,* and Michael Collier's *An Introduction to Grand Canyon Geology.*

the later Chuar, were laid down on top of the Vishnu to a tremendous thickness. They, too, were broken and tilted and lifted up into mountains. Up to 15,000 feet of rock was eroded away, leaving a low plain of Vishnu with scattered hills of Supergroup. Remnants of the Unkar Group outcrop widely in the eastern Grand Canyon from Nankoweap Canyon, mile 52, to Hance Canyon, mile 79. Thereafter, they appear intermittently westward, often in side canyons, such as at Bright Angel Canyon and Bass Canyon. Chuar Group fragments occur only in the eastern Grand Canyon between Nankoweap and Tanner Rapids, mile 68.5, and are not exposed at the river. The Unkar Group is composed of:

Bass Limestone: Grayish dolomite and metamorphosed shale that erodes to form a ledgy cliff. It was deposited on tidal flats and in a shallow sea and contains the earliest record of life found in the Grand Canyon—fossilized algae which appear in thin mounds called *stromatolites.*

Hakatai Shale: Vivid red-orange shale with minor beds of sandstone, which erodes to form slopes and benches. It often has raindrop and ripple impressions and mud cracks.

Shinumo Quartzite: Purple, red, white, and brown sandstones that erode to form a massive, mostly purple-brown cliff.

Dox Sandstone: Reddish sandstones interbedded with shales that erode to form gentle hills and valleys. The Dox is the most massive formation in the Grand Canyon, other than the Vishnu Schist, which extends into the earth to unknown depths.

Cardenas Lavas: Dark brown to black basaltic rock that erodes to form cliffs on top of the Dox, caused by volcanic eruptions that poured lava and ash onto the land. Other flows erupted on the sea floor and intruded into the other strata, partially metamorphosing them, as is seen in the Hakatai Shale in Bass Canyon. Another example is at John Hance's asbestos mines, which are at the contact between the Bass Limestone and Cardenas intrusives.

Great Unconformity: The erosional gap of from 250 million to one billion years, depending on whether the next formation, the Tapeats Sandstone, rests atop members of the more recent Grand Canyon Supergroup (shorter gaps) or the ancient Vishnu plain (longest gap).

Tapeats Sandstone: Brown sandstone with extensive cross-bedding that erodes to form a cliff at the brink of the Inner Gorge. It was laid down beneath the shallow, turbulent coastal waters of an advancing sea and has trails made by trilobites.

Bright Angel Shale: Light green, tan, ocher, and purplish shales, sandstones, and sandy limestones. It erodes to form a gentle slope called the Tonto Plateau that goes from Red Canyon at mile 77 to Garnet Canyon at mile 114. Elsewhere it forms ledgy cliffs. The Bright Angel Shale was deposited in quiet waters farther offshore in the same sea that was responsible for the Tapeats Sandstone. It has fossil trilobites, brachiopods, and trails of marine animals.

Muav Limestone: Mottled gray limestone and some sandstones and shales, which erode to form a cliff with sandstone ledges and shale recesses. It was deposited offshore in a shallow sea and has some fossil trilobites and brachiopods.

Temple Butte Limestone: Limestone forming thin purplish out-crops in the eastern Canyon; dolomite (another kind of limestone) forming massive grayish cliffs in the western Grand Canyon. It was deposited in ancient undersea stream channels that were cut into the underlying Muav Limestone during a time of a shallow marine environment. The Temple Butte contains fossil armored plates of a primitive marine fish.

Redwall Limestone: Blue-gray limestone that erodes to form a sheer cliff, which is stained red by iron oxides washed down over it from above. The Redwall was deposited in a warm, shallow ocean and is abundant with marine fossils — sea lilies, corals, brachiopods, trilobites, clams, snails, fish, algae.

Supai Group: Deep red and red-brown sandstones interbedded with minor bands of conglomerates and shales, with minor units of tan-to-white limestone near the base of the group, and capped by a massive red-brown sandstone cliff known as the Esplanade. The Supai Group erodes to form cliffs and ledges. It was deposited in a low river-delta environment and contains marine fossils, terres-trial plants, and amphibian tracks.

Hermit Shale: Rust-red, fine-grained shaley siltstone with mud cracks. It erodes to form a slope. The Hermit Shale was deposited as the mud of a vast river floodplain that covered the Grand Canyon region. It contains tracks of amphibians and reptiles and fossil ferns and other terrestrial plants that suggest a semiarid environment of deposition.

Coconino Sandstone: Buff-colored sandstone with prominent wedge-shaped cross-bedding. It erodes to form a massive cliff. The Coconino was deposited as great windblown sand dunes in a desert environment. The sea that deposited the next formation, the Toroweap, cemented the sandstone beds together. The Coconino contains tracks of scorpions, insects, and lizards.

Toroweap Formation: Cream-to-tan-colored sandstones and limestones that look very much like the Kaibab Limestone above it. The Toroweap erodes into ledgy cliffs and slopes. It was deposited by a sea and contains fossil brachiopods, corals, mollusks, sea lilies, worms, and fish teeth.

Kaibab Limestone: Cream-to-tan-colored limestone that erodes to form cliffs. It was deposited by a warm, shallow sea and contains the same kinds of fossils as the Toroweap Formation. For geology buffs, Jim Ohlman offers this: "Kaibab Limestone contains chert, whereas Toroweap does not. Toroweap contains gypsum and dolomite, which Kaibab does not."

The Kaibab Limestone is the top stratum of the Grand Canyon, but it is by far not the most recent rock in the region. From 225 million to 65 million years ago, additional strata—4000 to 8000 feet of sandstones, limestones and shales—were deposited but were almost completely eroded away. During this time, tropical forests and coastal swamps covered the Grand Canyon region and dinosaurs lumbered across it.

Over the last 65 million years, most rock formation has resulted from the deposition of travertine (see description in chapter 3) and volcanic eruptions and lava flows in the western Grand Canyon. The flows filled side canyons and poured over the walls of the Inner Gorge, hardening into black basaltic curtains. Within the past million years, lava flows in the vicinity of mile 179 dammed the Inner Gorge. Estimates of the height of the dams vary from 600 to 1500 feet. The latter size would have created a lake extending all the way back to Lees Ferry. The Colorado River, which has only been cutting the Grand Canyon for the last six million years or so, over time formed its lake behind the dams, then poured over and cut through them, creating the biggest and most famous navigable rapids on the entire continent, Lava Falls, mile 179.5. Another, possibly even bigger rapids, Lava Cliff Rapids at mile 246, was formed in the same way as Lava Falls but now lies drowned under Lake Mead.

Trails Data

Here's a summary of data on the trails. It's important to remember that routes and conditions change with weather and erosion. *Always check with the BRO for up-to-date information on water availability and routes.* One or more quadrangle maps cover each of the trails. I recommend using the big USGS map, "Grand Canyon National Park and Vicinity," alone or with the quads, because it enables you to identify features that may lie outside the quads' areas.

If I had to list the South Rim trails in order of increasing difficulty *right now*, I'd rank them this way:

The Corridor (Bright Angel, South and North Kaibab) and Hualapai Canyon (Havasu) trails are the least difficult, but the South Kaibab shouldn't be climbed in summer. The Hermit and Grandview are good introductions to the unmaintained trails. South Bass is in fair condition but requires route-finding ability. Tanner also is in fair condition but seems endless and isn't recommended for summer. Boucher is difficult and long, and route-finding ability is needed in the Supai and the Redwall. New Hance is very difficult, even hazardous, with some route-finding ability needed.

It's customary in hiking guidebooks to give approximate hours to hike. I do this reluctantly, because trail and weather conditions change and hikers' abilities, stamina, and pack weight will affect progress. The times given here are broad, and my advice to hikers, if you haven't gotten the message in the book, is this:

(1) Drink a lot of water, but drink frequently and not more than

a cup or two at a time. Don't get bloated, as that may impede assimilation of fluids. Eat often, taking in carbohydrates and salts.

(2) Stop frequently to rest. Rest will flush ache-making toxins out of your muscles and give you a chance to look around you.

(3) Take your time. You'll enjoy the trip more, and that's what it's all about. Just make sure you start out early enough to reach your destination. In the words of Jim Ohlman, "We'll get there when we get there." Or, as backcountry ranger Libby Ellis puts it: "How fast one hikes the Canyon or how much mileage one puts in does not matter. It's the feeling that you gain from it that means more than anything."

Bright Angel Trail

Water: (1) Mile-and-a-half Resthouse, approximately May-October (check with BRO); potable.
(2) Three-mile Resthouse, approximately May-October (check with BRO); potable.
(3) Indian Gardens, fountain, year-round; potable.
(4) Colorado River, but best to use above mouth of Bright Angel Creek; purify.
(5) Bright Angel Campground, fountain, year-round; potable.

Note: Garden Creek and Pipe Creek are contaminated by sewage leachings and the mule corral at Indian Gardens. Only in the direst circumstances should one take water from them. Purify!

Minimum amount of water per person to take: In summer, start at the rim with a full quart and a couple of empties, if you want to start with a lighter pack. When you reach Indian Gardens, fill all three quarts for the rest of the descent. Take at least three quarts per person on the ascent from the river to Indian Gardens. After water is shut off at the two upper resthouses in the fall, carry a good two quarts between the rim and Indian Gardens, and the same down to the river.

Map: Bright Angel quad.
Trailhead: Just west of Bright Angel Lodge, next to Kolb Studio.

Rim elevation: 6860'.

Indian Gardens elevation: 3800' (3060' below rim).

Colorado River elevation at mouth of Pipe Creek: 2400' (4460' below rim).

Miles: Rim-Indian Gardens: 4.6

Indian Gardens-river: 3.2

River-Bright Angel Campground: 1.5

Total, rim-Bright Angel Campground: 9.3

BA Trailhead to North Rim: 23.5

Hours to hike: Rim-BA Campground: 5–6 down, 7–9 up.

South Kaibab Trail

Water: None along trail.

(1) Colorado River; purify.

(2) Bright Angel Campground; potable.

Minimum amount per person to take down the South Kaibab in summer: four quarts. If you're *determined* to go up it in summer, take six or seven quarts. You'll want extra to douse your hat, face, neck. This necessary added weight alone should persuade you to take the Bright Angel up instead!

Map: Bright Angel quad.

Trailhead: Along Yaki Point spur road (off East Rim Drive).

Rim elevation: 7200' (60' lower than Yaki Point).

River elevation: 2420' (4780' below rim).

Miles: 6.3 to the river and a half mile more from there to Bright Angel Campground and Phantom Ranch. South Kaibab trailhead to North Rim: about 21 miles.

Hours to hike: 3–4 to river, 7–8 up.

Hualapai Canyon Trail
(To Havasu Canyon)

Water: None at trailhead or along trail (unless a flash flood!). Potable water at fountain at campground; water in creek must be purified. Minimum amount per person to take one way to junction with Havasu Creek in summer: four quarts going down; five coming up.

Maps: Supai, Kanab Point, and Tuckup Canyon quads. The big GCNP and Vicinity map is less cumbersome.

Trailhead: Hualapai Hilltop. See chapter 3.

Rim elevation: 5200' at Hualapai Hilltop.

Supai Village elevation: 3195' (2005' below Hilltop).

Mooney Falls elevation: 2690' (2510' below Hilltop).

River elevation: 1840' (3360' below Hilltop).

Miles: Sources differ on the distances. Since all the trails in the Grand Canyon invariably feel longer than they are, precise measurements — which apparently don't exist, anyway — aren't important. Mileages given here were provided by the park service and the Havasupai Tourist Enterprise.

Hualapai Hilltop-junction with Havasu Canyon:	7.0
Hualapai Hilltop-Supai Village:	8.0
Supai Village-Navajo Falls:	1.5
Navajo Falls-Havasu Falls:	0.5
Havasu Falls-Mooney Falls:	1.0
Mooney Falls-Beaver Falls:	2.0+
Beaver Falls-river:	3.3
Hualapai Hilltop-Colorado River:	16.3; feels like 20

Hours to hike: Hilltop-Supai Village: 4–5 down, 6–7 up.

Hilltop-river: 8–12 down, 16–24 up.

Hermit Trail

Water: (1) Santa Maria Spring, 2 miles from rim; purify.

(2) Hermit Creek; purify.

(3) Colorado River; purify.

Note: There's also water at Dripping Springs, which is a side jaunt off the Hermit Trail. See description in chapter 1. *Four-mile Spring, shown on the topo map, no longer exists.*

Minimum amount per person to take one way in summer: four to five quarts going down; six coming up (or refill at Santa Maria Spring).

Map: Bright Angel Quad.
Trailhead: Hermits Rest at end of West Rim Drive.
Rim elevation: 6640' at Hermits Rest.
Hermit Creek (campground) elevation: 2800' (3840' below rim).
River elevation: 2400' (4240' below rim).
Miles: Rim-Hermit Creek: 7.0
    Creek-river: 1.5
Hours to hike: Rim-Hermit Creek: 5–6 down, 7–9 up.
    Creek-river: 1 down, 1½ up.

Grandview Trail

Water: None along trail. O'Neill Spring, shown on topo map off west side of Horseshoe Mesa, is dry. Miners Spring, shown as "Spring" on topo map, off east side of mesa, exists; very difficult, even hazardous, trail down Redwall to it; purify. Seasonal water at springs shown on map off west side of mesa in Cottonwood drainage; ask BRO; purify.

Minimum amount per person to take in summer: If you're doing a day hike on the mesa and don't plan to drop down to Miners Spring for water, carry six quarts for the day. For backpacks, make sure you'll have four to five quarts to take you from Miners Spring to Hance Rapids (Red Canyon), about 7.5 miles. There may be water enroute seasonally at Hance Creek, where the Tonto Trail intersects Hance. Check with BRO about water in Hance Creek if you plan to camp in Hance Canyon.

Maps: Vishnu Temple and Grandview Point quads.
Trailhead: Grandview Point, out East Rim Drive.
Rim elevation: 7400' at Grandview Point.
Horseshoe Mesa elevation: 4800' (2600' below rim).
Miners Spring elevation: 4400' (3000' below rim).
Miles: Rim-mesa: 3.0
    Mesa-Miners Spring: about 0.5
Hours to hike: Rim-mesa: 2 down, 3–4 up.
    Mesa-Miners Spring; 1 down, 1 up.

South Bass Trail

Water: (1) Seasonal pools in creekbed in lower Bass Canyon; alkaline taste; check with BRO; purify.

(2) Colorado River; purify. Read chapter 6 carefully for route to river.

Minimum amount per person to take one way in summer: five quarts down, six or more up. Cache water on Esplanade. Hang a supply of water and food at Bass Camp (rim). If weather causes the road to be mired, you'll need your cache while you wait for conditions to improve.

Map: Havasupai Point quad.
Trailhead: Bass Camp; detailed instructions from BRO.
Rim elevation: 6650'.
River elevation: 2250' (4400' below rim).
Miles: Rim-river: 7.0.
Hours to hike: 5–7 down, 7–9 up.

Tanner Trail

Water: None along trail. Colorado River only; purify. Minimum amount per person to take one way in *springtime* or *fall:* Start with seven quarts and possibly one empty container. Cache two or three above the Redwall, depending on how fast you're drinking till that point. Remember, you'll need more water as you go lower and for the trip out. Coming out, start with three or four quarts, filling your spare container if necessary. If you're determined to hike the Tanner in summer (approximately mid-May through September), start at the rim with eight or nine quarts plus an empty and cache three or four. The river runners call this part of the Canyon "Furnace Flats" with very good reason!

Map: Vishnu Temple quad.
Trailhead: Lipan Point, out East Rim Drive.
Rim elevation: 7300'.
River elevation: 2700' (4600' below rim).
Miles: About 9; feels like 12.
Hours to hike: 6–7 down, 7–9 up.

Boucher Trail

Water: (1) Dripping Springs: 0.5 miles up from the junction of the
  Dripping Springs Trail and the Boucher. (This is out of
  the way if you've started at Hermits Rest.) Purify.
  (2) Boucher Creek; purify.
  (3) Colorado River; purify.

  Minimum amount per person to take one way to Boucher
  Creek in summer: six quarts down, a good seven coming up.

Map: Bright Angel quad and the big GCNP and Vicinity map for
  the topographic picture of the area. *The Boucher Trail is not shown
  on either map.* It is shown on the BRO's Backcountry Trip Planner
  map, in the Thybony hiking guide, and in chapter 4 of this book.
Trailhead: Hermits Rest.
Rim elevation: 6640' at Hermits Rest.
Boucher Creek elevation at Tonto Trail intersection (camp): 2800'
  (3840' below rim).
River elevation: 2325' (4515' below rim).
Miles: Hermits Rest-Boucher Creek: 9.3
  Creek-river: 1.9
Hours to hike: Hermits Rest-Boucher Creek: 7–9 down, 10–13 up.
  Creek-river: 1+ down, 1½+ up.

New Hance Trail

Water: None along trail. Possible seasonal pools in Red Canyon
  above where trail intersects creekbed, above a cottonwood
  tree. You may have to dig for it. Check with BRO on this
  possible source. Don't waste energy trying to find it. Water
  at Colorado River; purify.

  Minimum amount per person to take one way in summer:
  five quarts going down, six coming up.

Maps: Vishnu Temple and Grandview Point quads.
Trailhead: White-gravel widening of shoulder of East Rim Drive,
  4.8 miles east of Grandview Point turn-in or 1 mile southwest of
  Moran Point turn-in; three "No Parking Tow Away" signs.

Rim elevation: 7000'.
River elevation: 2608' (4392' below rim).
Miles: Rim-river: about 7; feels like 9.
Hours to hike: Rim-river: 6–7 down, 8+ up.

Tonto Trail

Almost all the books to date have given 72 miles as the Tonto's overall length, but it's longer than that. The park service has wheeled it out at 35.7 miles from Red Canyon to Indian Gardens, and 59.35 miles from Indian Gardens to Garnet Canyon, for a total of 95.05 miles. It's amusing to see a figure to the one-hundredth of a mile, and even that one shouldn't be taken too seriously. As Jim Ohlman says, "It's possible for two hikers to hike the Tonto differently and come up with a total distance of anywhere from 85 to 95 miles. It depends, too, on how often you lose the trail, say, between Slate and Garnet. Anyway," Jim concludes, "individual hiking time is more important than actual distance."

Here are approximate mileages based on figures from the park service and Jim:

Red Canyon-Hance Canyon	7.0
Hance Canyon-Cottonwood Canyon	4.0
Cottonwood-South Kaibab Trail	20.0
South Kaibab-Indian Gardens	4.1
Indian Gardens-Horn Creek	2.5
Horn Creek-Salt Creek	4.8
Salt Creek-Monument Creek	3.4
Monument Creek-Hermit Creek	3.5
(Some say the Indian Gardens-Hermit distance is 12. Expect 14.)	
Hermit Creek-Boucher Creek	5.5+
Boucher Creek-Slate Creek	4.9
Slate Creek-Bass Canyon	20.0+
Bass Canyon-Garnet Canyon	10–12.0
	Total about 90.0

Always check with BRO on seasonal water availability at springs and drainages enroute.

Beamer Trail

A trail with some washouts, above and along the Colorado River, approximately 9 miles from the Little Colorado River to Tanner Rapids. Check with BRO for information on where trail is near river for water. Purify.

Escalante Route

Cairned route above and along the river, approximately 10 miles from Tanner Rapids to Hance Rapids (Red Canyon). This route is not to be confused with the Escalante–Dominguez Route in the Lees Ferry area. Check with BRO for details on route and water.

APPENDIX C

Day Hikes and Rim Walks

Any of the South Rim trails can be hiked part way—permits are not required for day hikes—but some offer better day hikes than others. The New Hance and Hualapai Canyon trails, for example, would not be good choices, the New Hance because of its difficulty, the Hualapai because of its distance from Grand Canyon Village and its lack of any real midway destination. The Tonto Trail is too far away from the rim. All the other trails offer fine day hiking, and I give suggestions here, along with pleasant rim walks. Park rangers also lead interpretive walks. Check with the visitors center for schedules.

If you're going into the Canyon, take water, water treatment tablets (if needed), map, emergency kit, camera, snack, sunglasses, and appropriate clothing, and wear head covering. Expect the climb out to take up to twice as long as the descent, and make sure someone on the rim knows where you're going and when you expect to return.

Day Hikes Inside the Canyon

Bright Angel Trail (described in chapter 5). To One-and-a-half and Three-mile resthouses; potable water in summer. To Indian Gardens, 9 miles round trip, about 6 hours; potable water year round. For persons in good physical condition: to Plateau Point,

12 miles round trip, 8–9 hours; potable water at resthouses in summer and at Indian Gardens year round.

South Kaibab Trail (described in chapter 5). To Cedar Ridge, 3 miles round trip, 3 hours; no water. Here's an ambitious loop for persons in excellent physical condition: down the South Kaibab to the Tonto Trail, west on the Tonto Trail to Indian Gardens, and out the Bright Angel; 13 miles in all, 9–10 hours; no water until Indian Gardens. The 4.1 miles on the Tonto Trail are extremely hot in summer, with no shade. Carry five or more quarts of water per person to Indian Gardens, and drink it. Do not do this loop in reverse in summer, as the South Kaibab Trail is very steep and lacks water or shade, and you'd need to carry six quarts from Indian Gardens. Anyway, the terrific views from the South Kaibab are best seen as you descend it.

Hermit Trail (described in chapter 1). To Santa Maria Spring, about 4 miles round trip, 4 hours; water at spring; purify Waldron Trail, 6 miles round trip, 6 hours; no water. To Dripping Springs, about 6 miles round trip, 6–7 hours; water at Dripping Springs; purify.

Boucher Trail (described in chapter 4). For strong hikers: out to Yuma Point for the spectacular view of Canyon and Inner Gorge, about 10 miles round trip, 7–8 hours. Water only at Dripping Springs, a side jaunt of a half mile from the junction of the Boucher Trail with the Dripping Springs Trail; purify.

Grandview Trail (described in chapter 2). To Horseshoe Mesa, 6 miles round trip, plus exploring mileage on mesa; 5–6 hours. No water on mesa; very difficult, even hazardous, trail to Miners Spring at base of Redwall on east side of mesa; purify. O'Neill Spring, shown on map off west side of mesa, is dry.

Tanner Trail (described in chapter 7). To 75-mile Saddle, 3 miles round trip, 3 hours; no water. To the top-of-the-Redwall overlook as described in chapter 7, about 8 miles round-trip, 6–7 hours; no water. Carry six quarts for the day.

South Bass Trail (described in chapter 6). To the Esplanade, about 4 miles round trip, 3–4 hours; no water. If weather is doubtful, don't go, as rain or snow may make the rough dirt road to Bass Camp impassable. Hang supply of water and food at Bass Camp, just in case, and have gear that could get you through a delay until conditions improve.

Walks on the South Rim

Rim Trail. From Mather Point to Hermits Rest, 9 miles one way, nearly level; potable water at Yavapai Point and at Grand Canyon Village enroute; soft drinks for purchase at Hermits Rest. Paved stretch of trail between Yavapai Point and Maricopa Point. The summertime shuttle bus stops at major points along the way. Self-guiding nature trail pamphlets for sections of the trail are available at the visitors center and the museum at Yavapai Point.

Desert View Nature Trail. A fifteen-minute walk from the Watchtower to the campground; potable water at each end.

Tusayan Ruin. A twenty-minute walk through the ruins of an 800-year-old Indian settlement. Tusayan Ruin is located 4 miles west of Desert View, off the south side of the East Rim Drive (Hwy. 64). Museum, potable water and restrooms; ranger on duty.

APPENDIX D

Glossary

Abbreviations: BA – Bright Angel
BRO – Backcountry Reservations Office
CCC – Civilian Conservation Corps
GCNP – Grand Canyon National Park
NHA – (Grand Canyon) Natural History Association
NPS – National Park Service
USDI – United States Department of the Interior
USGS – United States Geological Survey

Alcove: A small, rounded recess or niche in a cliff wall; a small *bay*.

Amphitheater: A large, rounded, arenalike recess in a cliff wall. In the Grand Canyon, these can be very large to huge. An amphitheater is larger than a *bay*, and a bay is larger than an *alcove*.

Basin: A region drained by a single river system. See also *drainage*.

Bay: A recess in a wall or cliff that is larger than an *alcove* and smaller than an *amphitheater*.

Brachiopod: Clamlike shellfish with two differently shaped valves, or shells. Clams have mirror-image shells.

Break: An eroded section of a cliff that allows passage down and up it.

Burro: A small *donkey*, especially one used as a pack animal, native to North Africa. A *donkey* is a domesticated ass. An *ass* is a hoofed mammal related to horses. A *mule* is a sterile hybrid of a male ass and a female horse.

Butte: A freestanding feature with steep sides all around it; a small *mesa*. A butte has a generally vertical outline. Wotans Throne is a large butte with a flat top (a small mesa). Coronado, Cardenas, and Escalante buttes have irregular, even mountain-like tops. A *tower* is a butte that is taller than it is wide and is blunt across its top, such as Scylla Butte. See also *mesa* and *peak*.

Cairn: Pronounced like "care" with an "n" at the end. A pile of rocks marking a trail or route. Can be a few rocks or many rocks. See also *duck*.

Cliffwash: Dark streaks down a cliff face, caused by leaching of over-lying vegetation.

Community: An association of plants and animals occurring in a particular *habitat*. See also *habitat* and *life zone*.

Contour: Noun: a line on a *topographic map* that follows the same elevation above sea level. Verb: to walk along the same eleva-tion, as to contour around a hill. See also *quadrangle* and *topographic map*.

Diurnal: Active during the daytime.

Drainage: An area drained by a stream system. It may be small or large, and there are many associated terms. For example, Hermit Creek drains the *runoff* going into Hermit Gorge. The Colo-rado River system drains a 242,000-square-mile *basin* in parts of Wyoming, Colorado, Utah, Arizona, New Mexico, Nevada, and California—including the waters of its *tributary* stream, Hermit Creek. Some tributaries are *perennial* (always flowing), like Hermit and Bright Angel creeks; others are *intermittent*, or *seasonal*, like Slate Creek. A *branch*, *arm*, or *fork* is a smaller segment feeding into a tributary, as do the west and east arms of Tanner Canyon. A *wash* is a tributary or section of a tribu-tary that is usually or predominantly dry, like the wash leading up to Miners Spring.

Donkey: See under *burro*.

Duck: A *cairn* consisting of only two rocks. See also *cairn*.

Electrolytes: Minerals circulating in the blood that are essential to maintaining metabolic and muscle function. They include sodium (especially as combined with chloride in normal table salt), potassium, and magnesium.

Fault: A break or disturbance in the earth's crust caused by pres-sure and/or tension within the crust.

Geology: The science that deals with the origin, history, and structure of the earth.

Graben: Pronounced "*grah*-ben." A depressed area between two *faults*, such as the lava graben at Tanner Rapids, chapter 7. See also *fault*.

Habitat: A place where specific types of plants and animals tend to live. Plant habitats are determined by climate, soil, topography, and available water. Animal habitats are influenced by the food and shelter available there. All the plants and animals found in a particular habitat are called a *community*. See also *community* and *life zone*.

Igneous: As in *igneous rock*: a solidified, once-molten rock. See also *metamorphic* and *sedimentary*.

Intermittent: Off-and-on; now-and-then—i.e., seasonal. See also *drainage*.

Life zone: The plants and animals found in a certain elevational belt. At different elevations, climate varies and thus determines the kinds of plants and animals that will thrive there. A good discussion of life zones in the Grand Canyon can be found in Stephen Whitney's *A Field Guide to the Grand Canyon*, chapter 5. See also *community* and *habitat*.

Mesa: Any table land. See also *butte* and *peak*.

Metamorphic: As in *metamorphic rock*: a "changed rock," one which started out as an *igneous* or *sedimentary* rock and was later altered by heat and/or pressure. See also *igneous* and *sedimentary*.

Microclimate: An area with a climate different from the predominant climate of the region in which it lies, such as the cooler, moister microclimates containing Douglas fir in the Grand Canyon.

Mule: See under *burro*.

Nocturnal: Active by night.

Outcrop: A portion of bedrock or other rock formation protruding above or through the soil level.

Peak: A *butte* that is taller than it is wide and comes to a definite single point, like Vishnu Temple. A *spire* is a sharp peak, and a *pinnacle* is a very small spire. See also *butte* and *mesa*.

Quadrangle or Quad: An area of land represented on a *topographic map*, as in a quadrangle map. Quads usually are 15-minute size ("minute" here is a unit of space, not of time), covering an area of about 13 miles by 17 miles. 7½-minute maps, four to each 15-minute area, may have more detail. The USGS is developing 7½-minute maps for the Grand Canyon and may have some published within five years. See also *topographic map*.

Riparian: Of, on, or pertaining to the bank of a river, creek, pond, or small lake.

Runoff: Water flowing on ground surface that drains into a *drainage*. See also *drainage*.

Saddle: A low spot on a ridge connecting two higher elevations; a saddlelike depression in the ridge of a hill.

Scree: Loose rock on a slope; *talus*. Also used to describe loose rock along a steep trail. See also *talus*.

Sedimentary: As in *sedimentary rock*: any inorganic debris deposited by wind, water, or glaciers, which eventually becomes hardened into rock. See also *igneous* and *metamorphic*.

Seep: A spot where water trickles out of the rock or ground.

Spring: Water emerging from an underground source in small or large flow.

Stratum: Plural *strata*. A bed or layer of rock having the same composition throughout; a formation containing a number of beds or layers of rock of the same kind of material.

Switchback: Noun: zigzag trail construction down a slope or broken cliff to make walking easier and retard erosion. Verb: to zigzag down or up a slope or cliff. A very long zig or zag is more of a *traverse*. See also *traverse*.

Talus: Pronounced "*tay*-lus"; plural *taluses*. A slope at the base of a cliff formed by erosional debris from that cliff.

Topography: The relief and contour of the land surface.

Topographic map: Map representing all the surface features of an area by *contour* lines and a system of symbols. See also *contour* and *quadrangle*.

Traverse: Verb: to go up, down, along, or across a slope at an angle. Noun: a passing across, over, or through. Contrasts with *contour*, which is a staying at the same elevation. See also *switchback*.

Tributary: A stream or river flowing into a larger stream or river. See also *drainage*.

Trilobite: Tiny horseshoe crablike arthropod without the tail. Arthropods are invertebrate organisms having a horny, segmented external covering and jointed limbs. Examples are the insects, myriapods (like centipedes), crustaceans (lobsters, shrimps, crabs), and arachnids (spiders, scorpions, mites, and ticks).

Unconformity: A break in the sequence of older and younger rock formations, caused by the eroding away of some of the older rocks before those of a later (younger, more recent) time were laid down. There are unconformities between many of the formations in the Grand Canyon, but the longest gap is that of the Great Unconformity, as described in chapter 1 and appendix A.

Wash: See under *drainage*.

APPENDIX E

Addresses

NOTE: *Arizona is on Mountain Standard Time all year.*

General Information on Grand Canyon National Park

Grand Canyon National Park
Box 129
Grand Canyon, AZ 86023
602/638-7888

Backcountry Reservations and Information

Backcountry Reservations Office
Grand Canyon National Park
Box 1520
Grand Canyon, AZ 86023

Information phone line: 602/638-2474, Monday through Friday, 11 A.M.–5 P.M. (MST). Tape recording other times. Permits required for camping; not required for day hiking. Reservations must be made by mail or in person; none made by telephone. BRO sends a complete Backcountry Trip Planning Packet. Weather and trail condition information: 602/638-2245.

Lodging Inside Grand Canyon National Park at South Rim and at Phantom Ranch

Grand Canyon National Park Lodges
Box 699
Grand Canyon, AZ 86023
602/638-2401

Lodging Outside the Park

There are accommodations outside the park at Tusayan (not the same as Tusayan Ruin), 6 miles south of Grand Canyon Village on the South Entrance Road (Hwy. 64). The airport is located 1 mile farther south.

Havasu Canyon

Campground reservations:
Havasupai Tourist Enterprise
Supai, AZ 86435
602/448-2121

Lodge and hostel reservations:
Havasupai Lodges
Supai, AZ 86435
602/448-2111

Publications and Topographic Maps on the Grand Canyon

Grand Canyon Natural History Association
Grand Canyon National Park
Box 399
Grand Canyon, AZ 86023
602/638-7774

The NHA's publications catalog is available on request. There's a 20 percent discount on purchases for members. Membership form is printed in the publications catalog.

Topographic Maps Only

United States Geological Survey
Western Distribution Branch
Box 25286
Denver Federal Center
Denver, CO 80225
303/236-7477

Ask also for their topographic map symbols interpretation sheet.

Commercially Guided Hikes

Grand Canyon Trail Guides
Box 735
Grand Canyon, AZ 86023
602/638-2391

APPENDIX F

References

Maps

"Backcountry Trip Planner: A Hiker's Guide to Grand Canyon National Park." U.S. Dept. of Interior/National Park Service. Undated. Included in Backcountry Trip Planning Packet from BRO.

"Geologic Map of the Eastern Part of GCNP, Arizona." Prepared by William Breed, Peter Huntoon, and George Billingsley. Williams and Heintz Map Corporation, Washington, D.C. 20027, 1980 ed. Available from Grand Canyon Natural History Association.

"Grand Canyon National Park and Vicinity, Arizona." Topographic map. USDI/USGS, 1962. Available from NHA and Denver Federal Center (see appendix E).

"Grand Canyon National Park Backcountry Use Area Map." USDI/NPS drawing #113-60345, August 28, 1982. Included with the Backcountry Management Plan of August 1983.

"Guide to Indian Country." Automobile Club of Southern California, March 1980.

Quads: Bright Angel, AZ, 1962; Havasupai Point, AZ, 1962; Supai, AZ, 1962; Vishnu Temple, AZ, 1962. All from USDI/USGS and available from NHA and Denver Federal Center (see appendix E).

"South Rim" and "South Rim Village"—both on one sheet. Handed out at entrance stations to park.

Books

Abbey, Edward. *Desert Solitaire: A Season in the Wilderness.* Ballantine Books, New York, 1968.

Babbitt, Bruce, ed. *Grand Canyon: An Anthology.* Northland Press, Flagstaff, Arizona, 1978.

Blaustein, John and Edward Abbey. *The Hidden Canyon: A River Journey.* Penguin Books, New York, 1977.

Butchart, Harvey. *Grand Canyon Treks.* La Siesta Press, Glendale, California, 1970. Also recommended: *Grand Canyon Treks II* and *Grand Canyon Treks III,* La Siesta.

Butterfield, Bob and Backcountry Reservations Office. *Hiking the Inner Canyon: A Guide.* Grand Canyon Natural History Association, Grand Canyon, Arizona. No copyright date; predates Thybony 1980 guide.

Collier, Michael. *An Introduction to Grand Canyon Geology.* NHA, Grand Canyon, 1980.

Collins, Robert O. and Roderick Nash. *The Big Drops: Ten Legendary Rapids.* Sierra Club Books, San Francisco, California, 1978.

Fletcher, Colin. *The Man Who Walked Through Time.* Vintage Books paperback edition, New York, 1971. Original copyright 1967, Alfred A. Knopf, Inc., New York.

Goldstein, Milton. *The Magnificent West: Grand Canyon.* Bonanza Books, New York, 1980.

Hart, John. *Walking Softly in the Wilderness: The Sierra Club Guide to Backpacking.* Sierra Club Books, San Francisco, California, 1977.

Hirst, Stephen. *Life in a Narrow Place: The Havasupai of the Grand Canyon.* David McKay Company, New York, 1976.

Hughes, J. Donald. *In the House of Stone and Light: A Human History of the Grand Canyon.* NHA, Grand Canyon, 1978.

James, George Wharton. *In and Around the Grand Canyon.* Little, Brown and Company, Inc., Boston, 1900.

Loving, Nancy J. *Along the Rim: A Road Guide to the South Rim of Grand Canyon.* NHA, Grand Canyon, 1981.

Maurer, Stephen G., based on conversations with William G. Bass. *Solitude & Sunshine: Images of a Grand Canyon Childhood.* Pruett Publishing Company, Boulder, Colorado, 1983.

Morris, Larry A. *Hiking the Grand Canyon and Havasupai.* AZTEX Corporation, Tucson, Arizona, 1981.

Phillips, Arthur M., III. *Grand Canyon Wildflowers*. NHA, Grand Canyon, 1979.

Powell, John Wesley. *The Exploration of the Colorado River and Its Canyons*. Dover Publications, Inc., New York, 1961.

Priehs, T. J., ed. *The Mountain Lying Down: Views of the North Rim*. NHA, Grand Canyon, 1979.

Stevens, Larry. *The Colorado River in Grand Canyon: A Guide*. Red Lake Books, Flagstaff, Arizona, 1983.

Thybony, Scott. *A Guide to Hiking the Inner Canyon*. NHA, Grand Canyon, 1980.

Time-Life Books. *This Fabulous Century, Volume I, 1900–1910*. Time-Life Books, New York, revised 1978.

Wallace, Robert. *The Grand Canyon*. Time-Life Books, New York, 1972.

Wampler, Joseph. *Havasu Canyon: Gem of the Grand Canyon*. Howell-North Press, Berkeley, California, 1959.

Whitney, Stephen. *A Field Guide to the Grand Canyon*. Quill, New York, 1982.

Booklets and Leaflets

Berkowitz, Alan. *Bright Angel Grand Canyon Trail Guide*. NHA, Grand Canyon. No copyright date given.

———. *Guide to the North Kaibab Trail*. NHA, Grand Canyon, 1980.

Houk, Rose. *Guide to the South Kaibab Trail*. NHA, Grand Canyon, 1981.

NHA leaflets: *A Human Look: An Overview of Human History at Grand Canyon* (undated); *A Place for Everything: Life Zones and Ecosystems in Grand Canyon* (undated); *A Slice of Time: Geologic Eras of Grand Canyon* (undated); *Grand Canyon Climates* (undated); *Hiking the Bright Angel and Kaibab Trails*, 1982; *South Rim Day Hikes and Walks*, October 1983.

NPS leaflet: *Where Did the Energy Go?* (undated).

SAFECO Insurance Companies leaflet: *Think Hypothermia*, brochure taken from the film *By Nature's Rules* and published courtesy of SAFECO, Seattle, Washington, #AR-32 R1 2/73.

Articles and News Releases

Arizona Daily Sun. "Decision to Remove All Feral Burros Announced." Flagstaff, Arizona, May 21, 1980.

Avery, Ben. "Group Planning to Airlift Burros." *Arizona Republic*, June 5, 1980.

Harbster, David. "Scorpion!" *Backpacker* Magazine, May 1984, p. 8.

Ivins, Molly. "Wild Burros Plucked Out of Grand Canyon." *The New York Times*, Wed., July 30, 1980.

Mirkin, Gabe, M. D. "Eat, Drink and Be Merry—Especially If You Exercise." *Backpacker* Magazine, July 1983, p. 76.

NPS releases: "More Burros Removed from Grand Canyon," Jan. 26, 1981; "Grand Canyon Heading for Last Roundup," March 16, 1981; "Last Burros Removed from Grand Canyon," October 28, 1981.

Schroeder, John. "25 More Burros Caught by Cowboys in Canyon." *Arizona Republic*, October 22, 1980.

Scott, Sandra. "Transcanyon Pipeline." *Grand Canyon National Park The Guide*, Vol. VI, No. 6, May 30 through June 12, 1982.

Other

Brochure: *Havasu Canyon.* Mailed by Havasupai Tourist Enterprises, Supai, Arizona, 1984.

USDI/NPS. Backcountry Trip Planning Packet. GCNP, Box 129, Grand Canyon, Arizona 86023.

USDI/NPS. Backcountry Management Plan, August 1983. GCNP Resources Management Office, Box 129, Grand Canyon, Arizona 86023.

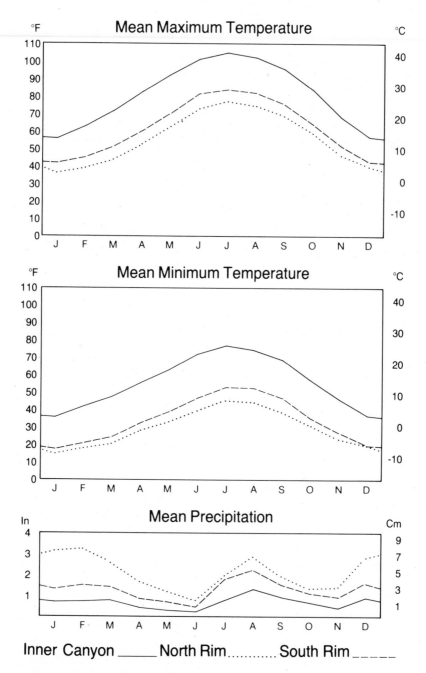

Mean Temperatures and Precipitation at Grand Canyon

APPENDIX G

Weather at Grand Canyon

NOTE: *See also entries under "weather" in the index.*

So far in our hiking, we've been fortunate with the weather, but in packing for every trip, we follow one unanimously endorsed piece of advice:
   Always be prepared for extremes, because Grand Canyon weather is unpredictable.

For us, being prepared means carrying layers of clothing suitable to our individual needs in seasonal extremes on the rim and inside the Canyon; having a waterproof, windproof outer garment and, in all but summertime, gloves and a wool cap; taking a tent; and having ice crampons or a walking stick for winter treks.

There are a couple of corollaries I'd add to the first piece of advice:

(1) *Always ask the BRO about current weather and its effects on water availability and trail conditions,* and

(2) *Heed the BRO's advice.* In summer 1986, for example, the monsoons didn't come, and parched hikers on the Tonto Plateau had to be rescued. The BRO had warned them that water sources were drying up, but they had insisted on going anyway.

These charts, courtesy of the Grand Canyon Natural History Association, show mean temperatures and precipitation for the North Rim, South Rim, and Inner Gorge. It's important to remember that temperatures and precipitation can vary widely from these means. Summertime highs at Phantom Ranch in the Inner Gorge have been recorded at 120 degrees Fahrenheit, lows at 50 (ripe temperature for hypothermia, especially if there's also rain and/or wind).

The Inner Gorge receives fewer hours of direct sunlight in winter than in summer, and although winter highs recorded at Phantom Ranch have reached 90, lows have dipped below zero.

Precipitation in the Inner Gorge during winter is usually in the form of rain, but it does occasionally snow there. Spring and fall can be capricious, especially on the rims—sunny and mild one day, moody and blustery (even snowy) the next. And the charts tell nothing about the winds and pelting sandstorms that can accompany weather systems or simply arise from the Canyon's topography and thermal conditions at any time of the year.

Our favorite times of the year to hike correspond pretty well with the moderate weather suggested by the charts: April-May and October-November. Upper reaches of South Rim trails may have ice and snow into April. The North Rim is closed from about November to mid-May because of snow (200 inches or more during winter is not uncommon).

INDEX

Sharon Spangler has worked as an English teacher, in public relations and journalism, and has taught hatha yoga. She has obedience-trained her three dogs, from left, Shadow, Sunshine, and Mollie, all of whom she adopted from the Denver Dumb Friends League. Sharon lives in Denver, Colorado, and continues to hike the Grand Canyon.